My name is Callum Ormond.

I am sixteen

and I am a hunted fugitive . . .

CONSPIRACY 365

BOOK TEN: OCTOBER

To Georgia Gabrielle McDonald and Prue

Scholastic Australia
345 Pacific Highway
Lindfield NSW 2070
An imprint of Scholastic Australia Pty Limited
(ABN 11 000 614 577)
PO Box 579
Gosford NSW 2250
www.scholastic.com.au

Part of the Scholastic Group
Sydney • Auckland • New York • Toronto • London • Mexico City • New Delhi • Hong Kong • Buenos Aires • Puerto Rico

First published by Scholastic Australia in 2010.

Illustrations by Rebecca Young.

Graphics by Nicole Leary.

Cover design by Natalie Winter.
Cover photography: boy's face by Wendell Levi Teodoro (www.zeduce.org) © Scholastic Australia 2010; close-up of boy's face by Michael Bagnall © Scholastic Australia 2010; officers chasing suspect © Radius Images/Corbis; dog 1 and dog 2 © Zelenenkyy Yuriy/Shutterstock; house on fire © James Pierce/Shutterstock; explosion © Gershberg Yuri/Shutterstock.

National Library of Australia Cataloguing-in-Publication entry:
Lord, Gabrielle, 1946-
Conspiracy 365: October / Gabrielle Lord.
ISBN 978-1-74169-322-5 (pbk.)
A823.3

ISBN-13: 978-93-5103-684-5

Reprinted by Scholastic India Pvt. Ltd., September 2015, 2019

Printed at Shivam Offset Press, New Delhi.

CONSPIRACY 365

BOOK TEN: OCTOBER

GABRIELLE LORD

SCHOLASTIC
SYDNEY AUCKLAND NEW YORK TORONTO LONDON
NEW DELHI HONG KONG PUERTO RICO

PREVIOUSLY . . .

1 SEPTEMBER

Believing my sister has drowned, I pass out on the banks of Spindrift River. A dream of Gabbi suddenly becomes real—she's alive and she's awake! Sharkey, Boges, Winter and I drop her off at a nearby police station.

12 SEPTEMBER

A message about the Ormond Riddle, from the Keeper of Rare Books, Dublin, convinces me I need to go to Ireland. In the meantime, with Boges's help, I make plans to spy on Oriana de la Force to get information on the whereabouts of the Jewel and the Riddle.

17 SEPTEMBER

Winter and I search through Sligo's car yard for the wreck of the car that killed her parents. Just as Winter believes she's found it, we are sprung by Zombie Two, and barely get out of there alive.

18 SEPTEMBER

In search of a safe place to stay, I go to see Repro.

20 SEPTEMBER

I steal Ryan Spencer's bus pass and leave it for my mum in Rafe's letterbox with the words 'Who am I?' written on the back.

I return to Repro's to find Three-O waiting for me—ready to call the cops and claim his reward money. Repro's place has been exposed and trashed, and they've tied him up. Within minutes, I'm trussed up too. We manage to free ourselves and escape through an emergency tunnel that collapses and almost crushes the life out of us.

21 SEPTEMBER

Boges and I set up near Oriana's house, and using an air-rifle I shoot a 'mothified' listening bug into her study. From our post across the street, we overhear her talking about a lodgement with Zürich Bank—are the Riddle and the Jewel in a safety deposit box?

22 SEPTEMBER

Retrieving the contents of Oriana's safety deposit box seems impossible, knowing that access requires fingerprint recognition and a PIN. After some online research I decide to try and get Oriana's fingerprint so that Boges can make a duplicate.

29 SEPTEMBER

Winter and I successfully collect a copy of Oriana's fingerprint, but I'm caught by one of her thugs. After trying to choke me, Oriana sends me out into the desert—to Dingo Bones Valley—with Kelvin, who has been ordered to kill me. After long hours in the boot, Kelvin makes me get out and kneel on the ground. A shot rings out . . .

30 SEPTEMBER

I wake up lying face down in red dust. I'm aching and thirsty, but alive. I discover some mysterious letters and numbers written on my ankle—SDB 291245.

An old prospector picks me up and gives me life-saving water, before taking me to an eerie, isolated town. He and his friend convince me to stay for a night and catch a bus out in the morning, but I soon discover that they plan on turning me in to the police for the reward money! After a violent struggle, I run into the desert while the two bounty-hunting prospectors and their vicious dog—Sniffer—hunt me down.

1 OCTOBER

92 days to go . . .

12:06 am

I'd fled that house of horror in a flash, over the sagging barbed-wire fence and into the night.

I ran across the desert sand, kicking up a shadowy cloud behind me. I was spurred on by the bouncing beams of torchlight following me, Snake and Jacko's shouts and, even more terrifying, Sniffer's barking.

My legs and arms pumped, propelling me over the hard ground and past scattered pieces of corrugated iron and dried-up animal remains.

I didn't know how those two old guys were keeping up with me, but they were, and from the sound of Sniffer's barking, I could tell they were getting closer.

A shot rang out, and I dived to the ground. Was it a warning shot, or had they fired at me?

I spat dust out of my mouth, crawled to my feet and kept running.

I couldn't shake them off. The terrain was

changing as I ran, and now I was avoiding rocky outcrops and low bushes. I was desperate to find a way of throwing Sniffer off the track. If only I could find a waterway—a creek, or a stream, like I'd waded through at Blackwattle Creek—so the dog would lose my scent.

Who was I kidding? This was a desert. There were no rivers in this place.

12:17 am

The dog was gaining on me—they must have let him off his leash. I wasn't sure how far Snake or Jacko were trailing behind, but Sniffer had galloped ahead of them and his barking was getting louder and louder. I figured I only had seconds before he'd be able to pounce on me and rip me to shreds.

Panicking, I crashed straight into a dense, thorny bush.

I dived down and burrowed into the prickly leaves, wrenching my backpack behind me as I copped painful scratches all over. I huddled there in a small hollow, trying to catch my breath, my blood pounding in my veins. I had hoped, for a second, that maybe if I hid in this prickly bush, the dog would give up . . . but I knew there was no chance of that actually happening. I just didn't know what else to do. I couldn't outrun the dog.

Sniffer bounded right over to the bush.

I held my breath as his bulky head turned my way. His nose dropped to the floor, sniffing, leading him directly to me.

He put his head under the bush, avoiding the worst of the thorns, and started worming his way in.

'Go away, boy,' I begged softly, as his warm breath hit my cheek. 'Please, Sniffer, go away.'

His snout was just centimetres from me. I'd have to jump up and make another break for it, shove him out of the way and run—if he didn't rip my face off first.

Sniffer growled and I wriggled as far away from him as I could.

But then his snout suddenly disappeared.

I peered through the foliage and could just make out his shadowy silhouette against the deep darkness of the night. He was a couple of metres away, sitting back on his haunches. His bulky body was still, and he was silent. He knew I was there, but he was staying away.

Was he just waiting, like a marker, for his masters to catch up so that they could drag me out of the thorny bush themselves?

The gravelly voices of the men approached. They were still some distance away, but the beams of light from their torches were becoming brighter, lighting up dust and insects in the air. If I ran now I'd be clawed down in seconds.

I waited, tense and terrified. At any moment I expected the dog to explode into a barking frenzy.

'Sniffer,' I whispered. 'Please don't show them where I am. Please don't bark!'

He turned towards me and growled. A long line of drool hung from his mouth. He dashed over and started charging into the thorns again.

'No, please,' I begged, wishing I'd just kept quiet. 'Leave me alone. Go away!'

He pushed and shoved his way through the bush and right up to my face. I braced myself for a brutal attack, closing my eyes and gritting my teeth.

But instead of the sensation of teeth clamping down on me, I felt a wet, leathery lick run all the way up my face.

I froze. He nuzzled in further and continued licking the dusty sweat off my face.

When he stopped he gave a little grunt and then started to wriggle backwards, out from under the bush.

Finally clear, he bounded away from where I was hiding, barking as he ran through the desert. He was leading the bounty-hunting men with the shotgun and torches in another direction!

He hadn't given me away! The dog didn't blow my cover!

Huddled and shaking, I watched with relief as their torchlight snaked further and further from me. Maybe some dogs were better than humans at telling good from bad.

I stared up at the brilliant stars above me as Sniffer's barking faded into the distance. 'Good dog,' I whispered.

12:57 am

When all was quiet, and all signs of torchlight had disappeared, I crawled out from my prickly position. I tried to remember where the main road was, and started running for it. I just hoped my memory of the map in Jacko's general store was accurate enough.

1:20 am

I thought I'd heard something—the sound of a distant truck. Was I imagining it? I stopped, straining to listen, then I heard it again. It sounded like of one those huge semi-trailers that own the night roads, speeding along with a mind of their own.

I jogged until I could see a brilliant light on the horizon. After jogging a few more metres the powerful light divided in two—two blazing headlights. Finally the truck drove into full view, illuminating the darkness. I watched the lights continue along the roadway until they vanished across the landscape.

Where there was one, there would be more, but no matter how thirsty and tired I was, I wasn't about to risk taking a ride from *anyone*. I was just happy I was free, alive and had the road to help guide me home.

2:01 am

I ducked for cover as another truck thundered along the road. I'd been trying to stay out of sight, worried someone would spot me and recognise me, and also worried that Snake and Jacko had hit the road searching for me after their dog had failed to help them.

Once the truck had passed, I walked on. All I could think of was my thirst, and cool, clear water.

3:35 am

I wandered along near the highway, weakening with every step from exhaustion and dehydration.

The truck had almost reached me before I even noticed its headlights on my back. Fear of being spotted put a bomb under me. I ran and dived onto the ground and scrambled behind some boulders.

The unmistakable sound of huge pressure brakes being pulled, screeched into the air.

I'd been seen! He was pulling over!

The big rig veered to the side of the road and slowed to a stop. It was just metres from me.

Desperate, I looked around for somewhere better to hide, but I was in a bit of a clearing—there was nowhere to run for more cover!

The cabin door opened and the driver jumped down. Instinctively I reached for the handle of the knife and waited, tense with fear. I'd have to scare him off. But then instead of coming straight for me, the driver launched out of the truck and kept running, stopping only to awkwardly unzip his pants.

He was stopping for a pee!

I had to stop myself from laughing!

I looked back over at his truck and saw an opportunity to sneak a ride. In the soft glow of the rear parking lights, I could see a corner of the canvas on the back of the truck was loose, flapping in the breeze.

I ran to the opening and heaved myself under the loosened canvas flap.

I was in.

I crawled to my feet in the darkness and felt around, wondering what this guy was transporting.

As my eyes adjusted, I could not believe what I was seeing. I was surrounded by crates of clear plastic cylinders, filled with . . . *water*!

A truck full of *water*! I was in the back of a bottled water delivery truck!

The driver had returned to the cabin now and as he kicked the accelerator and the truck lurched forward I almost fell into a crate behind me. As I steadied myself and greedily used my knife to pop the cap off one of the big bottles, all I could do was grin.

11:40 am

As soon as the water delivery truck began slowing alongside a big office building on the outskirts of the city, I jumped out the back. The driver had unknowingly delivered me practically all the way to my destination.

'Is Winter OK?' I asked Boges, as soon as I'd found a public phone.

'She's fine, she's fine, but what happened to you? What did they do to you? Where are you?'

'I'm back.'

'Back from where?'

'The dead,' I said. 'Or, at least, that's where I would have come from if everything had gone *as planned*,' I said, thinking not only of the crooked old prospectors, but also of the evil Oriana de la

Force. 'Did Winter give you the handbag with Oriana's fingerprint on it?'

'Not only did she give it to me, but I've already been practising cyanoacrylate enhancement, in preparation.'

'Sounds fatal,' I said, happy my friends were so reliable, even when I wasn't around. We were lucky the bug we'd planted had caught Oriana talking about the Riddle being 'lodged' with Zürich Bank in the city, but now we had to pull off some very complicated biometric hacking. We had to fool Zürich Bank. How realistic were our plans? We were just a bunch of kids going up against a huge international financial institution.

'Do you reckon we can meet up at Winter's place?' I asked.

'Dude, I can only–'

'Hello?'

The phone had cut out. It beeped in my ear before the line went dead. I hung up and searched my pockets for more coins.

I was carrying a small fortune in gold nuggets, but I didn't have enough change to make another phone call! I had to find somewhere to charge my mobile phone.

On the opposite corner from the phone booth was a petrol station. I scanned the area, searching for a toilet sign.

Bingo! Down the right-hand side behind the tyre pumps and ice freezer was a bathroom door swinging open. I walked in hoping no-one would notice me.

The immaculate bathroom in the beachside mansion I'd come to love flashed into my mind as I took in my current petrol-station toilet surroundings. There were two toilets overflowing with toilet paper and who knows what else, the tiled floor was wet and muddy—or, at least, I hoped it was mud—and high on the graffiti-covered walls hung a dozen daddy-long-legs spiders.

I pounced on the power point under the sink and plugged my phone charger in. When I stood up, a dusty, sunburned face looked back at me from the mirror. For a guy who'd been left for dead in the desert and then barely escaped the clutches of two bounty hunters and their dog, I didn't look that bad.

I shook my hair out and washed my face, then as I lifted my hoodie off, something strange tightened on my neck. When I reached in to feel what was pulling on me, my fingers touched a piece of fabric. Curious, I pulled it out.

It was Oriana's leopard-print scarf, the one she'd almost strangled me with! Somehow it had become caught around my neck and down the back of my hoodie, and had been there ever since!

My initial instinct was to ball it up and throw it in the bin, but then something seemed to tell me to hold on to it—that it might come in handy. I bent down and shoved it in my bag, brushing the leg of my pants in the process.

'SDB 291245' stared back at me from my exposed ankle. I rubbed at it again, but the marks wouldn't shift. What on earth could it mean?

12 Lesley Street

9:06 pm

Winter burst through her door and ran to me as soon as I reached the top of the stairs. She'd been busy studying with Miss Sparks, her tutor, and I'd been waiting downstairs for them to finish up. I was almost falling asleep against a brick wall when I finally saw Miss Sparks step onto the street with her bulky bag of books over her shoulder. As soon as she drove away in her little yellow hatchback, I headed upstairs.

'Cal!' said Winter, hugging me tight. 'I'm so sorry I couldn't let you in any sooner—Miss Sparks only just left.'

'Yeah, I know, I just saw her.'

'And I'm so, so sorry,' Winter added, 'I didn't know what to do when Sumo grabbed you. I hardly managed to get away myself—'

'Let's take it inside,' I said, grabbing her hand and leading her back into her flat. 'You did exactly what I wanted you to do. You protected the handbag with the fingerprint. Besides, you've saved me plenty of times already—it was about time I looked after myself. And here I am, safe and sound. Sort of,' I added, rubbing my throat. It was still aching from Oriana's attack and my struggle with Snake.

Winter ran to the couch and began picking up scattered textbooks that were flagged with tiny tabs of brightly-coloured papers, along with highlighters, black markers and notebooks. 'Here, sit down,' she said, gesturing to the cleared space, while awkwardly carrying everything over to her desk.

I grabbed a pillow from her bed and collapsed onto the couch. Immediately my eyes wanted to close. I tried to fight it and pay attention to what Winter was saying, but her voice was fading.

2 OCTOBER

91 days to go . . .

11:00 am

'What's that smell?' I asked, wincing in disgust. I struggled to sit up, wondering not only what the revolting smell was, but also what time it was.

'Boges, the boy wonder, has transformed my place into a laboratory,' Winter explained, looking up from a book she was reading.

'Boges? He's been here?'

'It's after eleven, Cal. You pretty much crashed out as soon as you stepped through my door last night! Boges turned up really early this morning and within ten minutes he'd turned my kitchen pantry into a fume cupboard. He's been experimenting with his own fingerprints and some foul-smelling glue.' Winter stood up and opened a window.

'Where is he now?' I asked, looking around the small place.

'He ducked out to get more superglue. He'll be back soon.' Winter suddenly stopped what she was doing and peered at me strangely. 'Oh my god,' she said, covering her mouth to stifle a laugh.

'What is it?'

'Oh, Boges,' she said, shaking her head.

'What is it?' I repeated.

'Go to the mirror.'

I jumped up and wandered to the bathroom, flicked on the light and stared at my reflection.

'I'm going to kill him,' I said, when I was met with not only a sunburned face, but a sunburned face with a black-marker curly moustache on my upper lip. 'It's not funny!'

11:23 am

After I'd cleaned up my face, Winter began taking me through the progress Boges had made so far. 'That's his own fingerprint,' she explained, pointing to the whorls and ridges of a fingerprint etched on a soft, malleable, transparent page. 'He put it through the process and came up with this.'

'It's awesome,' I said, lifting one of the transparent pieces and rubbing my forefinger over the print. 'I can actually feel the little ridges,' I said, looking up at her. 'They're pretty distinct.'

'Boges says it's good enough to fool the scanner on his computer.' I gave Winter a dubious look. 'However,' she added, 'the scanners at Zürich Bank may not be so easily convinced.'

A sound outside made us both jump.

'It's OK,' she said, looking out the window. 'It's just Boges.'

Winter opened the door and Boges stepped in with a parcel under his arm.

'I see you've shaved,' he joked, stroking his upper lip, and indicating the red strip on my face where I'd scrubbed off the moustache he'd drawn on me.

'You're lucky it washed off,' I said, thumping him playfully on the back. 'Unlike this,' I said, pulling up my jeans and pulling off my socks to show them my ankle.

SDB 291245

Boges and Winter stared at the letters and numbers on my skin.

'What is it?' asked Boges.

'Wish I knew,' I said. 'All I know is that after I was captured, Oriana wanted me dead. She ordered Kelvin to dump me in Dingo Bones Valley, which he did, but he obviously couldn't follow through on the "murder" part of her order because I woke up in the desert, alive. Then I found this on my ankle. I can't get it off. It's some kind of indelible ink—almost like a tattoo. I don't know why, but Kelvin must have done it.'

'SDB 291245,' Boges repeated. 'A phone number?' He pulled out his mobile and pressed the buttons. He put on the loudspeaker function and held up the handpiece.

'The number you have called is not connected,' recited the tinny voice. 'Please check the number and try again.'

'Could it be a birthday?' Winter suggested. 'Do you know anyone born on the 29th of December, 1945?'

I shook my head. The date meant nothing to me.

'Why would Kelvin mark you?' asked Boges, jotting down the letters and numbers in his bulging little notebook. 'It had to be him; unless some wandering desert nomad came across you lying unconscious and decided you needed cataloguing. But why?'

'I don't know, but the only reason I'm alive is because of Kelvin. He's a bad guy, don't get me wrong, but not a killer. Oriana's so cruel to him. Treats him like a dog. Worse than a dog,' I corrected. 'I don't know why *she* didn't finish me off when she had the chance.' I reached for my bag and pulled out her leopard-print scarf. 'She almost strangled me with this.'

Winter scrunched up her face as she took the scarf from me, holding it out at arm's length, like it was harbouring an infectious disease.

'So,' I said, turning to Boges, 'what do you have for us?'

'More glue,' he replied, sitting down and emptying the paper package. A couple of tubes fell onto the table. He picked up the soft, transparent paper with the print Winter had shown me. 'I did an impression, enhanced it with superglue to build up the loops and whorls of the fingerprint, and then I took a photo of the enhanced fingerprint and printed it off with really heavy contrast—to build up a thick layer.'

'And that process gives you the positive version again. Ready to press down on a scanner,' I said. 'Winter tells me that it's good enough to fool your PC, but will a copy of Oriana's fingerprint fool the scanner at Zürich Bank?'

Boges shrugged. 'Sounds crazy, but it's worth a try. We'll trim it down to size, then you need to wipe it over your skin for a moment or two, to pick up some body oil, then all you do is wear it over your own finger and press down on the scanner. It should work. In theory, at least.'

'I hate to be a downer, guys,' Winter interrupted, 'but even if the print works, we still have to get *into* the bank and access the scanner unchallenged. *And*, not only that, but we don't even have Oriana's personal identification number to get the security box open. Everyone has a PIN that they punch in to access their box in the vaults. The door won't swing open unless you have the right combination. Somehow we need to get Oriana's PIN.'

We stared at each other.

'We could capture her and torture her,' suggested Boges, breaking the silence. 'Force her to tell us the number.'

'Torture her?' scoffed Winter. 'Stoop to her level? Seriously, Boges, tell me you don't mean that?'

He shrugged.

'Don't forget the Piers Ormond will,' I said. 'It could have information in it that we need. We could still try and get our hands on that.'

'How do you propose to do that? Sheldrake Rathbone has doublecrossed you once already over that document. There's no way he'll just hand it to you. That's if he really even has it.'

I thought of my failed meeting with Rathbone at the funeral parlour, and the unknown assailant who'd jumped up and knocked me out, like some deadly jack-in-the-box. Rathbone was a dangerous enemy.

The three of us looked at each other hopelessly. I leaned on my knees and bumped my bulging pocket. 'Oh, yeah,' I said, digging deep into my jeans. 'I have something that should cheer us all up . . .'

Boges and Winter both leaned in, curious to see what I was about to show them. I pulled out a handful of gold nuggets and carefully let them fall on the table.

Boges blinked and Winter's hand flew to her mouth.

'What the?' Boges said, confused.

Winter picked up one of the gold pieces and glared at it closely, before turning to glare even more intensely at me. 'You have some serious explaining to do,' she demanded with a shove.

'Yes, dude,' Boges agreed. 'Before we spontaneously combust out of curiosity.'

'Not in here, thanks Bodhan,' said Winter, threatening to poke Boges with a fork. 'There's been enough combustion going on in my place this morning, thanks to you.'

Boges sprawled at the table and Winter sat cross-legged on her chair while I told them everything that had happened in Dingo Bones Valley. Boges's eyebrows almost touched his hairline as he listened. Winter seemed spellbound as I described how I got away from the demented prospectors, who planned to kidnap me and hold me until the cops came, all for the price on my head. I even added the bit about the rats in my room, and the bone I found that I suspected was human. When I told them about Sniffer, allegedly the best nose in the nation, and how he hadn't given me up, they were stunned into silence.

'There was a struggle in the kitchen,' I explained. 'Snake attacked me when I was trying to sneak out. He was going to rope me when the kitchen table came down on top of us, sending these guys,' I said, grabbing some of the gold, 'flying everywhere! He must have been counting his gold before I showed up downstairs. I grabbed as much as I could. They'd told me the gold had dried up.'

'Not true!' said Winter, examining one of the biggest pieces.

Boges shook his head. 'I've gotta tell you, man, you are one lucky dude!'

'Lucky? Me? Are you kidding? What about everything that's happened to me in the last nine months?'

'Boges is right,' Winter said, dropping the gold and sitting back in her chair. 'Well, I don't know if I'd call you "lucky" exactly, but while heaps of bad things happen to you, just as many good things happen! I mean, why didn't Kelvin kill you in the desert? Or why didn't Oriana strangle you to death? And how come that dog let you go? It was a *dog*. Can a dog really know right from wrong? Good from bad? And now you've returned with pockets full of gold! Someone's looking out for you. Someone's definitely looking out for you.'

'The Ormond Angel?' Boges suggested.

'I don't know about that,' I said. I didn't agree with what they were saying, but I couldn't help thinking of the water delivery truck that had appeared on the road like a mirage. That was pretty incredible.

Winter pulled a small, velvet pouch out of her drawer and tossed it to me. I started collecting up all of the gold from the table and the rest from my pockets.

'So anyway,' I said, 'what should I do with it?'

'I know a gold dealer,' Boges said. He took the pouch from me and weighed it up in his hands. 'Palladium Metal Traders. Uncle Vladi deals with them from time to time. A lot of people from the old country like to buy and sell gold. They don't trust money. I reckon you have about four thousand dollars' worth here. At least.'

I nearly choked on my own spit.

'Really?'

'At least,' he repeated, beaming. He wrote down the name and address for me on a piece of paper from his leather notebook and handed it to me. 'That reminds me,' he said, walking over to his bag and pulling out a folded piece of pink paper. 'This is for you. She said you'd know what it meant.'

4 OCTOBER

89 days to go . . .

Fit For Life

1:19 pm

Nelson Sharkey was wearing a sweaty grey tracksuit and a towel around his neck as we sat in the shade out the back of his gym. I'd done my best to get him up to speed on what had been going on with me. He offered me a sip of his blue sports drink.

'No, thanks,' I declined. 'There's something I need from Sheldrake Rathbone—the solicitor—and I know there's no way he'll give it to me willingly. Any suggestions?'

'You're not asking me to find someone to threaten him, are you?'

'No, I was thinking I'd need something over him. I guess I'm talking blackmail.'

Nelson considered what I'd said, and before long he was nodding.

'That might be possible. Rumours about him have run rampant for years. There have been allegations about funds going missing from elderly widows' trust funds, involvement in shady property dealings . . . But, of course, nothing's been proven.'

'But he *is* a criminal,' I said. 'I know that from my own dealings with him. He was part of a set-up that almost had me killed.'

'Was he?'

'What do you mean?'

'*Was he* part of the set-up? Look, I'm sure there's some truth to those rumours, but do you know that for sure? Sheldrake Rathbone may have been an unknowing pawn in someone else's game.'

I wasn't sure at all, but I found myself saying, 'He was definitely part of the set-up.'

'If someone's acting outside the law,' he said, 'and has been for a long time, then it's a part of their life.' Sharkey paused and skilfully pitched his empty bottle five or six metres into an open recycling bin. 'It's just a matter of catching them at it. That's the hard part.'

'Then I will watch him—like I've watched other people. See what he does, where he goes, who he meets up with—that sort of thing.'

'Exactly. You need to run a surveillance operation on him. If he's up to something, you'll catch him sooner or later.'

Palladium Metal Traders

2:53 pm

In a corner building, I found the sign I was looking for. I pressed the buzzer outside the glass door. The guy behind the counter looked me up and down before letting me in.

'How can I help you?' he asked. He had three gold teeth, a dark suit and a shoestring tie.

'I have some gold to sell.'

He leaned his head back, looking down at me with a superior sneer.

'Let's see it then,' he said.

I up-ended the velvet pouch, dropping the gold noisily onto the tray on the counter. I'd taken about half of it out and put it aside—I didn't want to cash all of it in right now.

I saw a flash of the gold teeth as the dealer smiled.

'You've been a lucky boy,' he said, hunched over my findings. 'Where have you been digging?'

'Dingo Bones Valley,' I said without hesitation. 'Maybe I've hit on Lasseter's Reef.'

His eyebrows shot up on hearing me mention 'Lasseter's Reef'. His eyes searched mine, examining me, while he rubbed some of the gold with a thin cloth. The nuggets gleamed brilliantly under the spotlights in the ceiling—some of them were rounded and smooth, others more jagged, pockmarked and uneven.

He snorted before pulling out his jeweller's loupe and squinting down through it at the collection of nuggets. He lifted the tray and poured them onto a small set of scales to weigh them, then straightened up and stared at me suspiciously.

'Well?' I prompted him, feeling uneasy under his intense gaze.

'I'll give you five hundred bucks for the lot.'

'*What?* Five hundred bucks? Are you kidding? That's robbery! This is worth over two thousand dollars,' I said, halving Boges's earlier estimation. 'I'm not stupid, I won't let you rip me off!'

The gold teeth flashed at me again. 'I don't believe you came across this gold honestly,' he said. He looked at me through his jeweller's loupe, wearing a crooked smile. 'You'll take what I give you, and count yourself lucky, kid.'

'You don't know what you're talk–'

'You're not fooling me,' he said, cutting me off. 'I can spot the difference between someone who's telling the truth and someone who's lying, like I can tell the difference between a cubic zirconium and a diamond. *You* didn't dig this gold out. Look at your hands–they haven't been swinging a pick or digging a mine. My bet is you knocked this off from someone. Take my offer or leave it.'

'I'll take it elsewhere,' I said.

'Suit yourself,' he said, dismissively. 'Good luck with that.'

'But there's easily two thousand dollars' worth of gold here,' I pleaded. 'You're not even offering *half*!'

'*Six* hundred bucks or I call the cops. There's something about you that makes me think you wouldn't like that very much.'

There was nothing I could do. He knew he had me. I couldn't risk this gold trader turning into another bounty hunter.

He folded up his loupe and tipped the gold from the scales back onto the tray. Next he reached for my velvet pouch.

'Deal,' I said, stopping him.

He counted cash from a red silk purse that had suddenly appeared in his hand. As he did that, I caught a whiff of that tantalising odour that I'd sniffed just before being knocked out at Rathbone's undertaking business. It seemed to be coming from behind a closed door, some way down from the counter.

'That smell,' I said, trying to source it, trying to work out what it was. 'What is it?'

With a deft movement, he swiped all the gold nuggets into a container under the counter, and flicked twelve fifty-dollar notes at me. 'Scram before I call the cops.'

5 OCTOBER

88 days to go . . .

12 Lesley Street

2:14 pm

After lunch, Winter and I had been throwing around ideas on how to catch Sheldrake Rathbone out on something scandalous—something worthy of blackmail.

A herd of zebras silently galloped across the tiny TV screen in the corner of the room. Winter was distracted by her textbooks. I knew school was tough enough on its own—it must have been really hard splitting her attention between the DMO and her study. I watched as she yawned loudly and let her head fall to rest on a pile of books on her desk.

I looked closely at the names of the books on their spines and saw that the one on top was a history of Queen Elizabeth the First.

Winter lifted her head and must have seen me squinting to read the cover.

'I'm wondering,' she mused, thoughtfully, 'whether Oriana is so desperate to understand the Ormond Singularity because she feels some weird, kindred connection to Queen Elizabeth. You know, they both share that "Off with his head!" sort of power. And it turns out "Oriana" was one of the names that Elizabethan poets and courtiers used to give Queen Elizabeth. Maybe Oriana thinks she's some kind of reincarnation.'

'She has the red hair, I guess.'

Winter turned away from her desk to face me, and folded her legs up on the chair. 'It's funny what motivates people, what drives them. Sligo wants to be respected and accepted by society, and Oriana—well, she already has both of those things. They both have money. They both have power. Some people are just never satisfied. They always want more.'

'Speaking of *more*, is there any more of that pumpkin soup from lunch?'

'In the fridge.'

I jumped up and headed over to the fridge, pulling a plastic container with orangey contents out.

'Want some?' I asked her.

'Sure,' she said, standing up and reaching for two small bowls from the sink. 'So, back to Rathbone. We all *know* he is a criminal, so maybe Sharkey is right. If we just run a surveillance operation on him we should catch him out doing something he shouldn't. Between the three of us—you, me and Boges—we should be able to cover a lot of his activities.'

'And then?'

'Then we get evidence and the blackmail begins.'

enhancement on target's fingerprint proceeding. 1st attempt a failure. starting from scratch.

'I hope he can do it,' said Winter, after reading Boges's message. 'At least he's found another place to use as a lab.' She leaned back in her chair to look at the clock on the wall. 'Miss Sparks will be back again tonight, don't forget.'

'I know,' I said. 'I'll clear out in a couple of hours and find a new hideout.'

Hideout
38 St Johns Street

7:46 pm

A temporary wire fence had been built around the property and on it hung a developer's notice. The doors and windows were boarded up and the overgrown yard was even thicker and wilder than before, creeping up the sides of the house like it was trying to swallow it whole.

I was up and over the fence pretty quickly, forging my way through the bushes and grass in the front yard. I listened carefully and looked for any signs of movement.

It was clear. I dropped to my knees and squeezed through the weeds under the front verandah, crawling beneath the house just like Boges and I had done months ago. The hole in the floorboards was still there although someone had nailed a couple of planks across it. I lay back on the ground, with my legs up, and kicked at the boards until they dislodged and came off. I hauled myself up into the familiar room.

Slivers of streetlight peeked through the cracks in the boarded-up windows. Someone had cleaned inside, swept the floors and ceilings clear of cobwebs, and removed all the rubbish and rotting furniture. The crumbling staircase had vanished entirely and in its place was a narrow ladder. I tested its sturdiness and carefully climbed up.

When my head was at the second-floor level, I peered around. The floorboards up there looked shaky, but the space was clear. There used to be a gaping hole in the roof where some tiles had broken and fallen away, but now it was covered with a blue-green plastic tarpaulin.

Back down the ladder, I checked the bathroom.

The broken sink was gone although the tap fittings and toilet were still there. Someone had gone to quite a bit of effort to clean up the place as best they could, yet it looked like no-one had been inside for quite a while. What had happened to the developers? Maybe they'd gone broke.

I decided to stay, for now, and remain on guard.

8 OCTOBER

85 days to go . . .

12 Lesley Street

7:20 am

We talked over our plans to coordinate the surveillance operation on Sheldrake Rathbone, dividing shifts between us, to cover both his house and his office. The small table was strewn with notes and piles of toast. In the corner, the TV flickered again with the sound off.

I picked up another piece of toast and smothered it in crunchy peanut butter. Boges nodded to me, indicating that he wanted one too.

Winter put down her toast and licked a drop of raspberry jam from her finger. 'Cal, if we're right about Rathbone–if he really is a crim–he could have some *big* secrets. Sligo-sized secrets. Look!' she said, suddenly distracted by the TV. 'Speaking of crims, look who's just appeared!' She hurdled over the couch to grab the TV remote, and turned the volume right up.

Oriana de la Force's unforgettable face filled the screen. She was almost as red with fury as her towering hair.

Winter put a finger to her lips.

'Police received an anonymous tip off,' said the newsreader, 'and are currently interviewing members of Ms de la Force's staff. Ms de la Force vigorously denies the charges.'

'This is outrageous!' screeched Oriana to the mob of microphones that circled her. 'I had nothing to do with the kidnapping of that Ormond child,' she spluttered. 'These ludicrous charges have been brought against me by a spiteful ex-employee. I am already mounting a counter-case against him for malicious prosecution and defamation. The child was kidnapped by her criminal brother, the infamous Callum Ormond. In fact, the police will most certainly be charging him with that offence as soon as he is brought back into custody.'

'Spiteful ex-employee?' asked Boges.

'Kelvin's dobbed her in,' said Winter. 'What's wrong with him? Does he want to lose his head? Look at her! Now she's so furious, she's turning purple! Her lipstick almost matches her face!'

'Kelvin?' I said. 'Could he be that mad with her? That bent on revenge?'

'Hate to break up the party,' said Boges, 'but I have to go. I'll organise a digital camera for you,

Cal, and I'll catch up with you outside Rathbone's office building after school.'

'Cool, thanks. I'd better head out, too. Start the surveillance.'

Winter went to one of the drawers in her dressing table and took out a small camera. 'Cal, for now you'd better take mine.'

Pacific Tower

12:09 pm

I'd been watching Rathbone's office building all morning, even though I was uneasy hanging around the city. I'd worked on my hair and clothes quite a bit and was counting on that being enough to escape detection. I'd also brought along a clipboard and a small parcel, hoping I could pass as a courier and get into the office.

Rathbone had entered the building around eight thirty, and he hadn't stepped back out yet.

1:11 pm

Just as I moved in closer to the foyer of the building, Rathbone appeared out of the lift. I quickly turned my head and pretended to look at the listing of business suites on the wall. 'Rathbone and Associates' was listed as being located in suite two, on level five. After a moment I turned around and saw my subject walking into a small sandwich bar and café next door.

From back outside I watched as Rathbone eventually re-entered the building and vanished into the lift, clutching a paper bag. Clearly he was taking his lunch up to his office.

4:33 pm

I was stoked to see Boges arrive on his bike.

'How's it going?' he asked, pulling his helmet off.

'Boring,' I said. 'Undercover work is not very exciting.'

'I can take over from here. You should get out of here before five o'clock. The less you're seen, the better. I know what Rathbone looks like and I know he drives a red Audi. I'll wait for him to leave and try and follow him home. I'll send you the address as soon as I can.'

'And then you'd better get back to perfecting Oriana's fingerprint.'

'Yes, boss!'

6:55 pm

r's address: 87 chesterfield ave, seaview heights. going home now.

Winter convinced me to grab a cab with her to Rathbone's. I had a bit of 'gold' money that I was happy enough to part with, so after about twenty minutes in front of the mirror—with Winter fiddling with my hair—we hopped in one from the closest rank and headed off.

The cabbie dropped us off a few blocks away from our destination and we made the rest of the way on foot.

87 Chesterfield Avenue
Seaview Heights

9:06 pm

The grey and white house was surrounded by lush lawns and gardens. A low hedge, trimmed meticulously, formed the front fence. A path led up to the entrance of the house, and a long driveway led to a triple garage. Beside the garage was a paved pathway to the backyard.

All was quiet.

We carefully crept up and peered down the side of the house. The edge of a paved terrace peeked out—a bit like the one at the back of Rafe's place. It also looked like he might have had a bit of a vegetable patch or something growing deep in the rear of the yard.

The house was shrouded in darkness. Not a single glimmer of light seemed to show from inside. It looked like whoever was inside was in bed and asleep. No point sticking around tonight.

Hideout
38 St Johns Street

11:21 pm

After Winter and I walked all the way back to her house, I decided to continue walking to St Johns Street. She told me Sligo had mentioned something about 'spending quality time' with her on the weekend, so I couldn't risk staying at her place, waiting for him to pop his nasty head through her door and find me on her couch.

And so I was back in the St Johns Street dump, feeling a great sense of déjà vu. Restless and trying to fall asleep on the creaking floorboards, my mind was skimming over everything that had happened to me since running into the crazy guy on New Year's Eve last year. The 365-day countdown was ticking away so fast. I'd come so far, but I still had so much to do.

I was thinking about some of the people who had helped me along the way—Jennifer Smith, Melba Snipe, Nelson Sharkey . . . and I was thinking about some of the people I hoped would help me in the future—Eric Blair, and the Keeper of Rare Books, Dr Theophilus Brinsley.

And then, of course, I was thinking about the guy who had my face. Ryan Spencer.

11 OCTOBER

82 days to go . . .

87 Chesterfield Avenue
Seaview Heights

8:09 pm

Boges, Winter and I had shared surveillance of Rathbone's house over the weekend, but none of us had uncovered anything worthy of blackmail—unless you count footage of Rathbone, when he thought no-one was watching, wandering out to collect the morning paper in his undies.

I was hoping this week would give us the breakthrough we needed, but today had been no better. I'd spent the day sitting outside Pacific Tower, watching the entrance while mindlessly scratching a thin layer of black colour off my mobile phone casing.

Now I was back at Chesterfield Avenue, hiding myself and Boges's bike in the bushes. The red Audi was parked in the driveway and a light was on upstairs.

I peered in the direction of the street when I heard footsteps walking up the path nearby.

I knew that silhouette anywhere. Winter.

'Hi,' she whispered, crouching down beside me. 'I know it's not my shift, but I needed a break from studying and thought you could do with some company–'

Winter suddenly stopped talking and pointed to the front door with her eyes.

It was Rathbone emerging, still in his suit and carrying a black briefcase. He fumbled with his keys before locking the door and heading for the driveway. The red Audi beeped, unlocked, and Rathbone climbed in and started the ignition.

'Quick,' I said. 'On the bike!'

Tartuffe's French Restaurant

8:32 pm

We looked through the vine-covered windows of the expensive city restaurant. Rathbone was sitting at a table in the corner with another man in a dark suit.

'That's not his usual briefcase,' whispered Winter.

'You're right,' I said, peering at the black bag at his feet. 'I've never seen that one before.'

We looked at each other for a moment before

Winter spoke again. 'Something different from the usual,' she said. 'It could mean something.'

I pulled out the camera Boges had given me on the weekend. I made sure the flash was switched off, pressed the lens to the glass and, when no-one was paying any attention, I took a picture.

I checked the image on the camera's screen. It wasn't a very clear shot, as the foreground was partially occupied by a couple near the window. But in the distance it showed Sheldrake Rathbone and his companion, and the black briefcase beneath the table.

'Look,' I said, noticing something else under the table as I zoomed in on the image. I turned the screen to Winter. 'The other guy has an almost identical bag at his feet.'

'So he does,' she said. I looked into Winter's dark, almond-shaped eyes. She suddenly squinted and grabbed the camera from me. 'Hey, wasn't that bag the one Rathbone went in with?'

'What?' I said, taking the camera back and looking at the image again. 'You think they've done a switch?'

'I swear he came out of his house with the bag that's now at the other guy's feet. It's more squarish than a typical briefcase. I could be wrong . . .'

'I think you're right!' I said.

87 Chesterfield Avenue
Seaview Heights

10:41 pm

Rathbone climbed out of his car, lugged the briefcase out after him, and returned to his house. Around us, the night was still and quiet, apart from a possum or two scurrying along the trees that lined the street.

'What should we do now?' I asked Winter. 'The briefcase is no use to us unless we find out what's inside it.'

'You want to break into his house?'

Before I could answer, Rathbone appeared at the front door carrying a small kerosene lamp in one hand and a shovel in the other. His eyes darted around the yard, a clear sign he was up to no good. He leaned the shovel against the wall and disappeared inside once more.

Winter and I grinned at each other, anxious to witness whatever was about to unfold.

A few minutes later he was back, this time with the black bag by his side. He reached for the shovel, turned on the lamp, and started for the backyard.

'You wanted *dirt*,' said Winter, 'and now it looks like you're gonna get it!'

We carefully followed Rathbone down the side

of the house. He went straight for the vegetable patch down the back. There seemed to be a few cabbages or something leafy growing in three neat lines, and beside that was a low mound of soil.

Rathbone stopped at the mound of dirt and placed the lamp on the ground. A small circle of light surrounded him. He pulled up his sleeves, took the shovel with both hands and began digging.

We huddled down behind a birdbath water feature that was flowing in the corner of the yard.

'He might be burying someone,' I quietly joked, as the sounds of the spade hitting dirt continued. Winter gave me a strange look, as if to say my words weren't that far-fetched. I shuddered, remembering my own burial at the hands of this shady guy we were watching.

The sound of digging became louder and then suddenly stopped. Had Rathbone sensed our presence? We squatted like statues, not daring to move.

After a moment I peered around the birdbath.

Rathbone was flat on his stomach, reaching into the hole he'd just dug. He grunted as if he were lifting something heavy.

He struggled, but finally squirmed backwards, pulling a wooden chest out of the earth. Rathbone knelt over it—it was about the size of a picnic esky—and wrenched the lid open.

Buried treasure?

Winter and I stared on, riveted. I was barely breathing as I watched him shuffle on his knees to the black briefcase. He looked at his left palm before running his thumbs over the twin number locks that clasped the bag shut. He must have written the code on his hand. The bag opened and he began lifting its contents out and transferring them to the chest.

'Cash!' Winter whispered. 'Wads of cash! Thousands and thousands of dollars!'

'Why would he bury money in his backyard?'

'Because he doesn't want anyone to know about it. He doesn't want the bank or the taxman to know about it, and he doesn't want anyone knowing *how* he got it!'

Silently I drew out my camera. Winter reached into her embroidered shoulder bag and pulled out her camera, too.

'Don't forget to switch off the flash,' I reminded her.

'Cal, we're gonna need it,' she said, as she squinted through the viewfinder.

She was right. It was too dark.

'OK, let's both take photos on the count of three, then run for our lives. Cool?'

'Let's do it!'

I zoomed in as far as possible.

'One,' I counted. In the tiny window, the figure of Sheldrake Rathbone, solicitor, stooped as he transferred the last of the wads of cash from the briefcase into the chest. 'Two . . . three!'

The night lit up with two camera flashes, one slightly later than the other, and then we were off, racing and tripping through the garden. I wrenched Boges's bike out from behind the bush and jumped on. Winter ran around in front and hitched herself up on the handlebars.

'Let's go!' she urged.

I pedalled like crazy, the bike flying down the footpath, carrying both of us. Winter's hair flapped wildly in front of me. She gripped the handlebars and risked an awkward twist around to give me a victorious grin.

12 OCTOBER

81 days to go . . .

12 Lesley Street

12:15 am

we busted rathbone big time! at winter's now.

Safely back at Winter's place we checked what we'd caught on camera. In my shot, Rathbone was stooped over in the act of putting something into the chest, but when I enlarged the picture, it was clear what he had in his hand—a very fat wad of fifty-dollar notes. Winter's shot, a second later than mine, had caught Rathbone's white face as he looked up, shocked and drained in the sudden flash of brilliant light.

When Winter enlarged her shot, it was clear that the dirt-covered wooden chest he'd unearthed already had a lot of cash packed in it.

'We got him! We got him!' we yelled, hugging each other and jigging around the tiny kitchen. We bumped into the couch and fell over backwards. Winter fell on top of me, but quickly jumped up.

She kissed her camera. We both knew that these photos meant we'd have the Piers Ormond will in our hands in no time.

u caught him doing what?! can't wait to find out! i'll call in on my way 2 school.

8:01 am

'Man, these are awesome! You have him red-handed. Where do you think he got all that cash?'

'Probably fleecing some poor old lady's trust fund,' I said, picturing a kind, elderly client of his, someone like Melba Snipe. 'All that matters,' I added, 'is that he's hiding money in a chest in his garden. It's gotta be dirty money. Honest people don't bank like that.'

'*Dirty* money,' Boges laughed. He pulled out his laptop. 'So let's send him one of them already—I think the one that shows his face will freak him out the most. I'll use one of my anonymous email addresses. We still have his email address from when he made contact on your blog ages ago. Do you have the camera cord for this?' he asked, picking up Winter's camera.

Winter fumbled through her desk drawer. 'Here it is,' she said, passing it to Boges.

'Just keep it anonymous for now,' I said. 'Let's make him nice and paranoid. I don't think he has a clue who was behind his birdbath last night. He'll be freaking out already.'

Boges transferred the photo from the camera to his laptop, then attached it to a blank email addressed to Rathbone. He nodded to us as he hit 'send'.

'All you have to do now,' said Boges, 'is wait. And then call him.'

'Awesome,' I said. 'I'll do it tomorrow. Let him stew for a day.'

13 OCTOBER

80 days to go . . .

Hideout
38 St Johns Street

9:40 am

'Sheldrake Rathbone,' he said, when he answered my call.

I deepened my voice, trying to sound tough like Nelson Sharkey. 'I believe you received an incriminating photo,' I said.

He was silent for a moment, and then I heard something like a door slamming. He was probably shutting his office door—he definitely wouldn't want anyone overhearing this conversation.

'Who are you? What do you want?' he growled into the phone. He was trying to sound threatening but I could hear the fear in his voice.

'You don't need to worry about who I am—what you need to worry about is that photo, or another one just like it, being handed over to the Law Society, the police or the press. Everyone will be wondering where Sheldrake Rathbone—a leading solicitor—got that briefcase full of money, and why he's burying the stash in his backyard?'

'You want money?' he blurted, clearly flustered and panicking. 'How much?'

'I don't want your money.'

'Well what *do* you want?'

'Something you promised me once before.'

'I don't know what you're talking about.'

'Let me make it a little clearer for you,' I offered. 'I want Piers Ormond's will.'

'I see,' he said, finally realising who his blackmailing caller was. 'The will in return for the photos.'

'That's correct. Give me the will and I won't distribute the photos.'

'And how will I know that you won't continue to blackmail me? Send the photos out after I've given you the will?'

'You won't know,' I said. 'Deal with it.'

His deep breathing puffed into the phone like a bull about to charge. But he knew he had no power in this. He knew I had him in a bind.

'Mr Rathbone,' I began, 'this time we'll meet on *my* turf and on *my* terms. I already have the photos of you in a draft email addressed to the Law Society, the police and all the key press players—they're ready to go, if needed. If you don't do exactly what I tell you to do, I will have someone send them out immediately.'

'When do you want to meet?' he murmured.

'Tonight.'

'Tonight? But that's impossible! I–'

'Tonight.' I repeated, firmly.

Rathbone inhaled and exhaled loudly. 'Where?'

I had the perfect place in mind. Somewhere I would feel comfortable, somewhere I could see him arrive and depart, somewhere Boges and Winter could also keep watch.

'Tell no-one about this meeting,' I said after giving him the details. 'Come alone. If you mess up and try something stupid, we'll put *you* six feet under.'

Crookwood Cemetery
First Avenue, Crookwood

9:00 pm

I knew Boges would be spooked, but Winter took it all in her stride. Boges was twisting on the spot, trying really hard not to look nervous, while Winter was sitting on top of a marble wall, swinging her legs and plaiting her hair. The three of us had met outside the Ormond Mausoleum early.

'So what's the plan?' asked Winter.

'Rathbone agreed to meet me here at eleven pm, sharp. I thought we should set ourselves up first, make sure he doesn't show up early to organise any interference. I've given him the directions to the Ormond Mausoleum. I'll be waiting for him right here.'

I turned to the door and noticed that the lock had been changed.

'I'll post myself outside the cemetery,' offered Boges. 'Near the entrance. I'll make sure no-one else shows up—no back-up, and more importantly, no cops. I can let you know exactly when he arrives. And,' he admitted, with a sheepish grin, 'it means I won't be on my own in here . . . This place seriously gives me the creeps!'

Winter giggled and even though it was dark, I was sure Boges was blushing. 'I'll hide somewhere over there,' she said, pointing up the path towards the entrance.

'Perfect,' I said. 'It will take him about five minutes to walk down to me.'

The three of us ducked and dived behind tombstones and statues as a security patrol suddenly approached.

Once it had passed, we all crept out of our hiding places. Boges was jumping about, frantically wriggling and brushing himself down, as though he was completely cocooned in spider webs.

Winter and I couldn't help ourselves—we both cracked up laughing.

10:51 pm

We were all in position and waiting for Rathbone to show up. Above me, on the stone façade of the mausoleum, on the lintel above the iron gates, faded gold lettering spelling out 'Ormond' was just discernible in the starlight. Despite the gloomy, quiet surroundings, the vandalised angels and broken columns sticking up from the graves like decaying teeth, I wasn't scared at all. I was so used to living in the dark that I almost felt at home back here at the place where my search had begun—with the discovery of Dad's drawings hidden inside the vault.

A faint sound in the direction of the main gates suddenly alerted me. I guessed it was Rathbone's car.

Boges was the first to message me:

📱 eagle has landed. approaching gates. alone.

Winter followed a minute or two later:

📱 he's walking down the path now. carrying torch. looks as scared as boges ☺

Rathbone's footsteps softly crunched down the gravel path. I was almost enjoying this. I hoped his guilty conscience was spooking him in this silent and solemn place. Behind me in the mausoleum lay the bones and ashes of my family, but I wasn't frightened of the dead. It was the living who were endangering me.

I pressed up against the mausoleum wall. I was calm and determined, my torch in my hand, imagining the courage of Captain Piers Ormond flowing in my bloodstream.

10:59 pm

Within the darkness of the footpath a thin beam of light shone. Rathbone's stooped silhouette followed behind it. With hesitant steps he emerged from the shadows and waved his torch over the tombstones and vaults, searching for the one titled 'Ormond'.

Once he spotted it, he slowly made his way closer until he was standing a metre or so from the steps that led up to the mausoleum door. I jumped down, deliberately scaring him.

He jumped back with a gasp.

'Mr Rathbone,' I said as he recovered himself. I shone my torch on him and saw an anxious man with dark circles under his eyes, flustered and afraid. He blinked and shielded his eyes with his hand. 'You have the will?' I asked.

He cleared his throat. 'What about the photos?'

'The will,' I insisted.

He tucked his torch under his arm and took

something from his pocket. 'Here,' he said.

I shone the torch on the document he had given me. On the front page I read in old-fashioned writing: 'Last Will & Testament of PIERS ORMOND, Gent. Regimental No. 1589 17th Battalion Imperial Forces. 15th September, 1914'.

This was it! The will I'd been after for so long!

I stepped back, pocketing it safely.

'The photos?' he asked.

'Last time you promised me this document it almost cost me my life.'

'What?' he asked, appearing confused. He straightened up. 'Surely you don't think I had anything to do with that? How dare you suggest I had anything to do with an attempt on your life!'

'You're the one who set up the meeting at your brother's funeral parlour,' I reminded him. 'I came, just like you asked–'

'It was not my fault the meeting went awry,' he said. 'The photos,' he hurried on, changing the subject. 'You have the will, now what about the–'

A night bird shrieked, making Rathbone jump again.

'You will never see the photos again and neither will anyone else,' I said. 'As long as you cause no further trouble to me.'

Rathbone's shoulders seemed to lower and relax on hearing this–his life and reputation weren't going to be ruined after all. He shook his head at me and turned to walk away.

A few steps up the path, he stopped and turned back. 'You don't know what you're up against, boy. You're just one kid, alone. My client is rich and powerful. What do you think you can do with that will?'

'That's none of your business,' I said, cringing at the thought of Oriana, thinking her wealth and power gave her the right to other people's property.

'I'm telling you this for your own good. You're in over your head. Whatever you think you're doing, you're never going to get away with it.'

'I'm not trying to get away with anything,' I said. 'I just want the truth.'

I heard him snort with contempt. 'There's no such thing as the truth,' he snapped. 'There are only opportunities, and the right moments to seize them.'

'My dad taught me differently,' I said. 'The truth will come out. It doesn't belong to *your client*.'

'Your father is dead. Why don't you give up and leave the Ormond Singularity to the people who are in a position to pursue it? Back out of this and you'll be left alone.' He took a step closer, speaking now in a softer, friendlier tone. 'I could make it worth your while—organise financing so that you could disappear and change your identity . . .'

'What a joke! I've already had to do that! There's no way I'm backing out! And unless your client is the *firstborn male* descended from a very particular family tree,' I pointed out, 'she has no right to it.'

'How can you talk about rights?' sneered Rathbone. 'You're just a pathetic, fugitive kid. A deadbeat criminal on the run. It's too late for you to start sounding like a boy scout. Don't you understand? You *have* no rights! But you can still save your life. Tell me you're backing out of this crazy dream of yours, and I can pass that on to my client. You want to live, don't you?'

I lunged forward and Rathbone backed away, suspicious.

'I believe that truth is something far more incredible than money and thuggery. It's power! Getting to the truth of the Ormond Singularity is my assignment. It was given to me by my family—handed on by my dad. There's no way I'm giving up. So pass that on to your client.'

Rathbone was silent.

'Get out of here!' I shouted.

Rathbone just stood there, unmoving.

'Go on, get out!' My shadow loomed over him like a huge wave about to fall.

'You're a fool,' he said, turning and walking away. 'They'll get you next time,' he called back before disappearing up the path.

14 OCTOBER

79 days to go . . .

12 Lesley Street

1:20 am

My friends sat silently at the table with me while I ran my eyes over Piers Ormond's will.

I skipped some of it because it was written in old-fashioned language. There were lots of numbered clauses about 'devising and bequeathing jewellery and possessions', as well as allocating a chestnut mare, Wilhelmina, to a foreman. I scanned impatiently until I finally came to the clause that I was looking for.

'Here's the bit about the Ormond Singularity,' I said.

'Go on, read it out,' urged Winter.

Clause 7: (iv) I give devise and bequeath to such child as is identified by my legal representatives my findings on the Ormond Singularity, provided that at the date of my death I myself have not discovered the benefits. I direct my legal representatives to convey to that beneficiary that such gift is his to pursue so long as it is accepted on the given conditions. Whoever should succeed to the Ormond Singularity must bequeath the Ormond Singularity to the firstborn child of the next generation carrying the name of Ormond up to and including the date of December 31st being a year of the double solar eclipses, after which the Singularity becomes void and empty, and all benefits, lands and deeds, entitlements, patents of nobility, gifts and treasures, and sundries all become null and void and revert in entirety to the Crown. (See Westminster 1285 'De Donis Conditionalibus')

'Translation, please?' I asked, putting the page down. 'Boges? Winter? Anybody?'

'There's a double solar eclipse this year!' said Boges, nodding. 'Dude, everything points to this year! He's talking about this year!'

'The crazy guy you met on New Year's Eve was right,' Winter added. 'The paperwork you found ages ago at Oriana's was right. It's all counting down to December 31st. This December 31st.' She shifted up onto her knees and leaned over to read through the will again. 'So the Ormond

Singularity can be handed down in a will, like it's something physical.'

'Exactly,' said Boges. 'Then if the person who inherits it is unable to claim what it offers–unable to work out the mystery of what the Ormond Singularity actually is, in their time–they have to hand it down to the next generation, to the next firstborn male.'

'Just like the family tree indicated,' I added. 'So all of my predecessors have failed to claim it, and now it's up to me. I have until December 31st to figure it all out. And then what? What happens at the end of the year?'

'Here, check this out,' said Winter.

Clause 8: I further direct my executor to inform such beneficiary of the Ormond Singularity as may be, that should no claimant for the Singularity arise by the stroke of midnight on December 31st, in the year of the double eclipses, then the benefits thereof wheresoever and howsoever situate, revert in entirety to the Crown in the person of King George V or his descendants as ordered by the Monarch in the 1559 codicil added to 'De Donis Conditionalibus,' dated 1285, the Ormond Singularity.

Piers Ormond, September 1914.

'If you don't uncover what it is,' said Winter, 'it's up to the Crown to work out. And if they don't know what they're searching for, it could all just crumble away.'

I stood up, frustrated. 'We still don't know what the Ormond Singularity means. What are we trying to uncover? What if we go to all this trouble only to find out it's nothing valuable, just some old piece of writing?'

'Don't be so impatient!' Winter said. 'Property and money—that's what wills are all about. My parents,' she paused, her voice wavering, 'left all their property and most of their money to Vulkan Sligo. On the proviso that he look after me.'

'She's right,' said Boges. 'Property and money. "Lands and deeds, entitlements, patents of nobility, gifts and treasures, and sundries",' he quoted. 'Your dad did say to you in his letter that you might have to get used to the idea of being seriously rich.'

I nodded to my friends. 'But we only have a couple more months to work it all out. Or we lose the lot. It goes to "the Crown". This is our last chance to keep it in the Ormond family. We have to get the Riddle and the Jewel back. We have to get into Zürich Bank.' I looked to Boges, hopefully.

'The print is almost ready,' he said, pausing to yawn. 'Give me another couple of days.'

17 OCTOBER

76 days to go . . .

Outside Zürich Bank

3:24 pm

Sheldrake Rathbone was out of the way, so we'd been focusing all of our energy on Oriana and our bank bust. This morning Boges had called to tell me he'd perfected the fingerprint, which was awesome news, but we still had a lot to work out before we could try using it. We still needed to successfully make it in and out. And, above all, we needed Oriana's PIN.

Winter and I were sharing surveillance shifts. Yesterday, Winter had posted herself at the bank, watching how people went in and out. If a client wanted to access the bank vaults, she watched how they paused at the scanner, pressing their fingerprint, waiting the few seconds until the physical barrier—two strong steel doors—released and they were allowed through.

It was during my surveillance shift that the

dark blue Mercedes pulled up outside the bank. I scuttled over the road with Boges's bike and watched from the park opposite. Oriana clawed her way out of the passenger seat, stood up, adjusted her white suit jacket, and smoothed down her skirt. Her flame of red hair was high, as usual, and her outfit was questionable, but immaculate. Her purple glasses sat atop her superior nose. Cyril the Sumo—who was looking rounder than ever—bounded over to her and walked beside her up the stairs and through the automatic glass doors of Zürich Bank. How she walked in those high heels, I had no idea.

I padlocked the bike and helmet and crossed the road. Keeping my face turned away from the security cameras, I followed her into the bank, pretending to take an interest in the pamphlets on student accounts. I swiftly pulled out my phone, switched on the video mode, and pressed record.

Carefully I filmed her, capturing her movements and her style. Once inside the bank's double glass doors, she swept straight over to the biometric scanner, pressed her forefinger over the sensitive area, barely waiting for the steel doors to open before disappearing through them. She didn't pause once to take off her sunglasses.

In only a couple of minutes, Oriana and Sumo reappeared in the bank foyer, talking with a clerk.

Oriana's voice was so loud and intense, it was like she was commanding everyone's attention.

I quickly pocketed my phone, ducked out the front doors and down the stairs, then across the road to my bike. I unlocked it, jumped on and started pedalling, heading for the corner. I was half-steering, half-pulling my helmet on when I collided with someone.

Down we crashed—me, the bike and the guy, as well as the three cardboard boxes he was carrying. The boxes spilled open and scattered their contents everywhere.

I twisted my legs out of the pedals and on all fours I began gathering up the stuff that had spilled—magazines, buttons, key rings . . .

'Sorry, sir,' I began, 'I didn't see you coming.'

'You!' he grizzled. 'I knew I'd *bump* into you again somewhere! Haven't you done enough damage to my property already?'

I looked up the skinny legs and folded arms in a too-short green suit, to find two big possum eyes staring into mine.

'Repro! I'm sorry, I didn't see you!'

I pulled my helmet off and quickly gathered up the rest of the bits and pieces that were strewn all over the footpath.

'I thought I was rid of you,' he said, as I stacked up the last of his boxes. 'And here you are, popping up again, or should I say, crashing into my world again! Quick,' he said, practically dragging me around the next corner and down an alley.

'How are you?' I asked tentatively. 'Where have you been staying?'

He shook his head at me and let out a big, frustrated sigh. He heaped two of the boxes on the front of my bike, so that he was left with just one in his own arms. 'Follow me.'

5:10 pm

Repro's new place was like an oversized, abandoned shed. It was less than ideal. For a start, there was no way to hide the front door and there were dozens of gaps in the roof and holes in the walls. I noticed the photo of his mother was hanging from a nail in the cracked wall. Her half smile seemed strangely familiar.

'You can't go on living here,' I said. 'This place must leak every time it rains. All your papers and journals would turn into papier-mâché.'

'Oh, don't you worry, this is only temporary,' he said. 'It took me ages to clear away the rockfall at my old place, just so I could get back in and collect my stuff. I have another lair lined up, I'm just using this for storage,' he said, looking around the place with his wiry hands on his hips. 'I could do with some help with the move.

I was just sitting here this morning, wondering how in the world I was going to manage shifting everything from here to my new place. It's funny,' he said, 'how help sometimes lands, quite literally, in your lap!'

I smiled, wishing he could also help me solve my problems.

'Because of the bluecoats and other nasty types, like those little thugs who trashed my collection and tied us up,' continued Repro, 'it's best to make the move to *the cavern* at night.' He looked at me as though he were waiting for an answer.

I knew I owed Repro. Big time. 'Of course I can help you,' I said. *The cavern* sounded interesting.

8:10 pm

We moved as Repro wished, under cover of night, using narrow old shafts and tunnels. I followed him with a heavy-duty torch, carting and hoisting boxes of his collection up and down a near-impossible path.

We finally stopped at a place where a tunnel widened out into a low-roofed cavern. Beyond the reach of our lights was blackness, darker than the darkest night. I had no idea what lay beyond, and didn't have much time to think about it—as soon as we laid our loads on the ground, Repro dusted off his hands and led us off again to fetch more.

It took us countless exhausting trips, hauling his remaining belongings, his dismantled bookshelves, the artworks, all the stuff that he'd collected over the decades. We retraced our steps through the tunnels, emerging in the cavern, and then back to the shed for yet more of his stuff.

10:12 pm

Finally, after lowering the last of the cartons down the shaft to where the rest of the collection was piled up in the cavern, Repro stopped. He stood his torch upright on the ground and sat on one of the boxes. I joined him, exhausted and relieved the job was done. We listened to the distant rumble of the trains through the rocks around us, and shivered in the chill of the air.

Once the rumbling passed, I became aware of the sound of dripping water. Plink, plink, plink . . . I picked up my torch and approached the pitch-black end of the cavern. What was beyond there, I wondered? More tunnels? A honeycomb of other, smaller caves? This place was more private for Repro than the shed, but it still wasn't what I imagined for his new home. It was too vast, too open.

'Take my torch, too,' said Repro, tossing it to me. 'You may as well check out the next part of the job.'

'*The next part?*' I asked, looking around at

the huge pile of stuff we had just moved over the last few hours.

'The night is young and we're already halfway.'

'Halfway!' I said, almost choking. Was this guy for real? Where were we headed, the centre of the earth?

I took the torch from him and went where he pointed, to the place where the blackness spread beyond us. I held the two torches high and they penetrated the inky wall of darkness.

'Oh man!' I gasped, shocked and amazed.

Close beside me, Repro chuckled. 'You didn't think you'd be going boating tonight did you?'

I stood gaping at what lay ahead. Black and rippling in the torchlight, beneath a continuation of the cavernous roof, stretched an endless underground lake. Stalactites from the ceiling dripped water onto its placid surface, making wide ripples in the water. A few metres to my right, on the shore of this amazing underground sea, a small wooden boat barely rocked.

'Come on. Don't just stand there like a galah. Give us a hand to load up the boat.'

10:33 pm

We piled cartons into the boat until the waterline was only a few centimetres below the prow. I steadied the small craft while Repro climbed on board, then I hopped in and used one of the oars to push off. I picked up the other oar and soon developed a steady rhythm, cutting through the dark and silent lake. Repro sat at the bow, shining the torch ahead.

'OK, navigator. Where to?' I asked.

'Straight ahead. To the other side. I'll give you plenty of warning before landfall.'

Repro's torch cut a narrow swathe of light ahead of us. It was an eerie trip, gliding across the black water, dipping the creaking oars into the surface and propelling us along.

I realised Repro was smiling proudly and looking at me as I took our surroundings in. 'You like it?' he asked.

'It's amazing,' I said. 'I've heard stories about a lake under the city, but never believed them!'

11:41 pm

Repro insisted on transporting everything over before he'd let me check out his new place. It took five trips there and back before we'd shifted all his stuff, and by that time, my arms were aching, my clothes were soaked and my sneakers were squelching, filled with water . . . but still, I couldn't wait to look around.

'I've been working on this site for a while now,' said Repro, hanging up a lamp, 'and already bought the conduit for the wiring down here. Another day or two and I'll have full power again. There's a sewer line just over there,' he said pointing to the side of the lake, 'and I'll build my bathroom on top of that. I'll add my little pipe in. No-one will even notice.'

We were in the dead end of a tunnel, that no-one else would probably ever realise existed. I looked around at the weird set-up, the harsh shadows cast over the walls and the water by the lamp.

'Another few weeks and you won't know the place,' Repro chuckled. 'There's plenty of air here and I'm even planning an open fireplace with the chimney running up one of those shafts. Imagine an open fire in the winter. With a bit of luck, Santa Claus might even visit me!'

It took a bit of imagination, but I was starting to picture some pretty cosy living quarters.

'I'll build a nice rock wall here,' Repro continued, pointing to the open end of the tunnel, 'and make another secret door.'

He dug out a packet of chocolate biscuits from a washing basket of stuff. 'Now, take a seat and have a break. No, not on that one. That's the box of track detonators. Don't want to set off an explosion!'

I kicked off my sneakers, rolled up my wet

jeans, and sat on another one of the upturned boxes. I grabbed a couple of biscuits and tucked into them.

'What's that?' Repro suddenly asked, looking at my legs.

'What's what?'

'The numbers. On the inside of your ankle?'

'I wish I knew,' I said.

Repro stared intently at the marks.

'How did they get there? Did *you* write them?'

'I'm pretty sure Kelvin put them there last month, after he dumped me in the desert. He'd been ordered to kill me, but he couldn't do it, and when I woke up I found them there. Won't rub off.'

Repro looked again at the fading numbers and letters. 'You know what it is, don't you?' he said. 'You know what those numbers mean, right?' He made it sound like only an idiot wouldn't know exactly what he was talking about. 'I suppose,' he said, rubbing his fingers together, 'the question is, *what's inside?*'

'I don't get it.'

Repro laughed, his eyes wide in disbelief.

'I wasn't the only lucky one today, my boy!' he said. 'You're just as lucky you ran into me!'

'Please,' I urged, 'just tell me what you're talking about.'

'Why would someone write the number of a safety deposit box on *your* ankle?'

'The number of a *what*?' I wasn't sure I'd heard him right. 'Did you say "safety deposit box"?'

'Sure did. That's what that is. SDB stands for "safety deposit box", and that's the PIN following it. Whose is it? Obviously not yours!' He cackled again with laughter.

The PIN! It had been with me, staring me in the face, all this time! Kelvin, who'd been told to kill me, not only spared my life but gave me access to Oriana's treasures!

Kelvin whom I'd saved from a bashing. Kelvin who was sick of Oriana's orders. Kelvin who'd informed the police of Oriana's involvement in Gabbi's kidnapping!

Did Kelvin hate her enough to betray her like this? Had he handed over her PIN to me in revenge? Or was it all part of an elaborate trap?

'Are you sure?' I asked.

'Of course I'm sure. I have an SDB myself at Zürich Bank. That surprises you, doesn't it?'

I jumped to my feet. 'Repro! I have to go!'

He looked up at me, his big, warm eyes shining by the light of the lamp.

'Repro, I could kiss you! Now how do I get out of here?'

18 OCTOBER

75 days to go . . .

12:11 am

boges, winter! this is HUGE! I have the PIN!

12 Lesley Street

12:54 am

Winter opened the door and her eyes searched mine, waiting for me to explain myself. She was wearing that oversized T-shirt she often wore to bed, and her hair was all over the place. Her eyes looked red, like she'd been rubbing them.

'Well?' she urged.

I sat down on the couch and lifted up my jeans, showing her my ankle.

Her mouth opened wide as she gasped. 'S. D. B,' Winter said slowly. 'Safety Deposit Box—and then the PIN! No way! Kelvin? He must despise that woman as much as we do to betray her like that!'

'I ran into Repro,' I explained. 'As soon as he

saw it, he identified it. He has a safety deposit box too!'

'So that's it! We have the fingerprint and now we have the PIN!'

'I have it all figured out,' I said. '*You're* going to impersonate Oriana.'

'*Me?* You're joking. I look about as much like Oriana de la Force as you look like that scrawny Griff Kirby.'

'Don't worry. We can fix that. Big, red hair, purple sunglasses. Bright lipstick. A stuffy suit. I know you can pull off that kind of staggering, leaning walk thing she does on her high heels.'

Winter went to her dressing-table drawer and pulled out a pair of huge sunglasses, putting them on. They hid the top half of her face.

'See, you're halfway there already! We're going to get into Zürich Bank and we're going to get back the Ormond Riddle and the Ormond Jewel!'

It was when Winter sat down beside me that I realised there were scrunched-up tissues all over the couch and floor.

'Hayfever,' she said.

'Since when do you suffer from hayfever?'

'Oh,' she sighed. 'I told you I can never get away with crying. It's just . . . I haven't been able to stop thinking about Mum and Dad's car at the car yard. I snuck back there the other day, to have a closer look at the wreck, but Zombie Two was on patrol.'

'We'll do it together,' I promised. 'I'm here to help you solve your mysteries, too, remember?'

'Thanks, Cal,' she said, standing up and kissing me on the forehead.

7:25 am

We hadn't been awake long but Winter had already pulled out some potential 'Oriana' clothes from her wardrobe. She skipped around and draped them over a chair, popping different pairs of shoes on the floor.

When we heard Boges puffing on the doorstep, we both looked at each other and wordlessly agreed. Winter disappeared into the bathroom, taking the clothes with her.

Boges knocked. 'Wakey wakey, you two,' he called.

'Hang on!' I said, waiting by the door for Winter to emerge. Her hand snaked around the wall, reaching for a lipstick from a small make-up bag.

'Almost ready,' she whispered.

She stepped out and did a little twirl. She was wearing a white blazer, a straight, knee-length black skirt, white high heels, a red scarf around her head to give the effect of Oriana's hair, bright lipstick, and huge sunglasses.

I gave her the thumbs up and opened the door.

Boges stood in the doorway, his face white with shock.

Then he had a closer look at the tall red-head with the sunglasses and purple lipstick who stood in Winter's flat, and cracked up laughing. 'Awesome!' he said.

I slapped him on the back. 'That's how we're getting into Zürich Bank. That's how we're going to get the Riddle and the Jewel back! And this,' I said, kicking my ankle out into his view, 'is the magic PIN we thought we were missing!'

'I've always wanted to impersonate a homicidal criminal lawyer,' said Winter, posing with a pencil, sucking on it dramatically like it was one of Oriana's cigarillos. She leaned back and almost fell over, balancing awkwardly in the high heels. 'Oops!' she said, kicking them off. 'They were my mum's—I'm not used to wearing heels!'

7:46 am

Boges and Winter watched the video from Zürich Bank on my phone. 'The thing that really stands out,' I said, 'is how nobody gives them a second glance. They are obviously a very familiar sight at the bank.'

'So I guess you're about to tell me I'll be playing the role of the sumo wrestler?' Boges asked.

'You won't even have to shave your head!' I pleaded.

Boges stood still, tolerating me while I began stuffing his football jersey with some of Winter's shawls and scarves.

'Now put your jacket back on,' Winter ordered in a loud, intimidating voice–she was already impersonating Oriana.

With his jacket back on, over the padding, Boges looked seriously round. He checked himself out in the mirror.

'Cool,' I said. 'Now all you have to do is borrow a suit jacket from one of your uncles, and put on your mirrored sunglasses.'

Boges looked thoughtful all of a sudden. 'I think I can rig up a sound system that will keep us in contact with you. Leave it with me. Anyway, help me get this stuff out will you?' he said, pulling a long cashmere scarf out from his sleeve. 'There's no way I can rock up to school like this.'

20 OCTOBER

73 days to go . . .

12 Lesley Street

4:32 pm

'You'll be operating the two-way,' explained Boges, as we went over the technical side of our bank bust plan. 'I'll wear this connector—a little earbud on an almost invisible cable that'll tuck under my collar. You'll be in radio contact with us throughout the bust, so if anything happens and we have to get out of there fast, you'll know about it.'

Winter caught my eye. She was twirling her hair into a bun on top of her head, preparing to pull on an incredible red wig she'd picked up at a market stall.

'This is the radio,' Boges explained, handing me the larger of the two devices he was holding. 'You can contact me and I can talk back to you, using this.' He patted the radio connector that was now hidden inside his jacket pocket. 'Switch it on, dude. Let's test it.'

I walked outside, hurrying over to the furthest end of the flat roof. Above me the sky was blue and the city lay spread around, a faint haze above it. A crow squawked from a nearby television antenna. 'Can you hear me, Boges?'

His voice came through the radio receiver in my hand. 'Affirmative.'

'And I have you, loud and clear, Boges.'

'Let's hope it works as well in the bank,' said Boges, as I walked back inside the flat. 'I'm just not sure what sort of interference we might get.'

We recited Oriana's personal identification number over and over again until we all knew it off by heart, and we went over the layout of the bank, so that Boges and Winter could sweep in confidently, just like the people they were impersonating.

Next, we studied the footage I'd taken. Sumo had a way of holding his arms stiffly out by his sides, and Oriana's unique lean-back style of walking in her stilettos wasn't difficult for Winter to mimic, once she'd mastered the art of the heels.

'How's this?' asked Boges, lumbering back and forth across the small flat, with his shirt stuffed and his arms held out in Sumo's odd way.

Winter loped along beside him, her hips leading her.

'Well!' she screeched, again doing her best to

impersonate Oriana. 'You heard him! Tell us what you think! Don't just stand there like a stunned mullet! Answer me!'

'That's creepily convincing!' I admitted, squirming in my seat. She'd pinned the red hair up perfectly, just like Oriana, and had that ferocious, unrelenting look in her eyes.

'What about me?' Boges suddenly demanded, in his best Sumo impersonation. 'I'm talking to you, buster!'

I grinned at my two deceptive friends. 'You've both nailed it!' I said proudly. I was starting to feel pretty good about our chances. 'OK guys,' I said, as Boges prepared to leave. 'Let's do it. Tomorrow.'

21 OCTOBER

72 days to go . . .

7:40 am

I didn't sleep very well on Winter's couch. I woke up every couple of hours, tormenting myself with the 'what ifs'. What if the radio failed? What if the fake fingerprint didn't work? What if my friends were sprung?

Boges arrived, just as nervous and excited as me. Winter disappeared to get ready.

'Wow!' I said, when Winter emerged in full costume. She wore a tight purple suit, red patent-leather high heels, a huge pair of sunglasses with leopard-print frames, and a silver handbag. A delicate scarf was wrapped around her elaborately styled red hair.

'Spitting image,' added Boges, as he bulked up his own outfit. With his crew cut, mirrored sunglasses hiding his eyes, and his suit jacket bulging, he seemed to have grown taller as well.

'I borrowed Uncle Vladi's boots,' he explained, showing them off.

'The heels are almost as high as mine!' scoffed Winter.

Boges dug into his school bag and pulled out the two-way radio. He popped the earpiece into his ear, pulled the transparent cable down under his collar, and slipped the small radio connector into the inside pocket of his suit coat.

Very carefully, with tweezers, he drew out a small object from a little plastic box. 'And here's the fingerprint,' he announced.

Winter looked mesmerised. 'It fits perfectly,' she said, slipping it over her forefinger. It was almost invisible and covered her own fingertip completely.

'Looks like all systems are go,' I said.

Outside Zürich Bank

10:02 am

I stood outside, near the road, watching my friends—'Oriana' and 'Cyril'—approach the steps of the bank. Winter walked with an odd gait, exactly like Oriana, and Boges lumbered beside her as Sumo, suitably hulking and menacing.

They charged through the automatic doors, striding in as if they owned the bank. They walked straight past reception and the teller counter, heading towards the biometric scanner.

I was tense and edgy, leaning on a bus stop bench, trying to look inconspicuous. I was constantly scanning the street for unexpected dangers.

Boges's voice in my ear made me jump.

'So far, so good, dude,' he whispered, his voice crackling just slightly. 'We're coming up to the first big hurdle.'

From what I could see, nobody in the bank had given them a second look. They swept towards the furthest corner where the biometric scanner was.

This was the moment. I could just make them out, pausing as they approached the scanner. Blood pumped in my temples.

Right now, Winter would be steadily pressing her finger—with its tiny transparency over it—down onto the sensitive reader.

I held my breath.

I heard a dull beep and hoped it wasn't an error reading.

Boges swore in my ear.

'Try again,' I hissed, keeping my head down, pretending to talk on my mobile phone.

The dull beep sounded again.

'It's not working!' he said. I could hear the distress and despair in his voice. 'I don't know why, but it's not working!'

I turned away, closing my eyes in disbelief. We

couldn't let all our hard work go to waste. 'Get out of there,' I hissed. 'All is not lost. You just have to make another fingerprint. We can do it again. Just get out of there before you blow your cover.'

There was no answer. I looked back into the bank and blinked. I couldn't see them. Had they been stopped? Were they being arrested?

I ran up to the bank's double doors, which parted as I approached.

They were on the other side of the scanner! Quickly I retreated to the bus stop.

'We're through!' came Boges's voice, finally. 'Took us three attempts—wow, that was intense! I thought the machine was going to swallow her finger or something! Like the ATM does to your bank card if you get the PIN wrong too many times!'

On my portable radio I could hear their footsteps echoing on the hard surface of the floor. I pictured my friends on their way to the security boxes.

'We're walking along a wide, marble hallway,' whispered Boges. 'It's incredible. On each side there are hundreds—maybe thousands—of safety deposit boxes. Big ones at floor level, smaller ones as you go up the wall to the ceiling. The first two numbers of the PIN—29—seem to refer to boxes—

they're all numbered. We're trying to find box 29. We're not game to ask anyone for—'

Suddenly there was silence and my heart froze. *What was happening?*

I could hear the sudden scuff of feet coming to a stop. I strained to listen harder.

Winter's voice screeched into my ear: 'Watch where you're going!' she yelled at someone who must have bumped into her in the hallway.

'Terribly sorry, Ma'am,' came an unknown voice.

I slumped with relief. That was exactly the sort of thing Oriana would have said to someone stepping in her way. Winter had nailed it, again.

'Sorry about the interruption, dude,' whispered Boges. 'We're still trying to find the box. There are guards patrolling up and down this corridor, but they don't seem to be taking much notice of us. We're approaching the lower numbers now. Box 29 shouldn't be far away.'

I could hear Boges, but his voice was breaking up. 'We've . . . SDB . . . 29. She's . . . key . . . numbers . . . now.'

'Boges,' I said, 'there's some kind of interference. I can't hear you properly.'

As I looked around, wondering what the interference might be, I got the shock of my life. The dark blue Mercedes screeched to a halt outside of the bank.

It couldn't be! But it was! The worst possible thing that could happen was actually happening! I scuttled out of sight.

The real Oriana de la Force appeared, swinging her legs in their purple heels out of the car and onto the footpath. Cyril the Sumo, unapologetically parking in the No Standing zone in front of the bank, lurched out of his door, straightened his jacket, ran his fingers over his crew cut, and slammed the door of the car.

Immediately, I turned away. I couldn't run the risk of being recognised.

'It's working!' I heard Winter's excited voice come through my earpiece. 'It's working!'

'It's opening!' I heard Boges say. 'We have the box open!'

'Guys!' I hissed. 'Get out of there! Grab the contents and get out of there!'

'There's a packet in here!' Boges said, too distracted to hear my warning.

I raised my voice, speaking between gritted teeth. 'Listen to me! You've gotta get out right now!' I commanded, desperation rising as I saw Oriana and Sumo scaling the bank stairs. 'Grab the stuff and get out! Oriana and Sumo are outside! Any second now they'll be walking into you!'

'What?'

'You heard me!' I stared through the glass.

The real Oriana and Sumo sauntered towards the scanner.

I grasped the radio with clammy hands. If Winter and Boges walked out now, wearing their Oriana and Sumo outfits, they would practically collide with their real-life counterparts and all hell would break loose!

Oriana and Sumo had stopped short of the door. They seemed to be deep in a massive argument. She turned to Sumo with one hand on her hip, and jabbed an accusing finger at him with the other. He was visibly upset, puffing up his chest and shouting back at her.

I looked past them, through the glass windows, and saw Winter and Boges, still wearing their fake outfits, hurrying towards the entrance foyer. Any second now and they would walk straight into the two criminals they were impersonating!

I snatched up the radio connector but didn't have time to warn them again—they were already walking out.

A few metres ahead of them, Oriana and Sumo were still arguing fiercely. *Don't turn around*, I willed the feuding pair. *Don't look behind you!*

Rigid with tension I watched the scene unfold.

Boges and Winter only hesitated a second before walking through the automatic doors. They looked horrified when they saw the two familiar figures just ahead of them, but they quickly veered to their right, out the doors, and scuttled away unseen.

At that moment, Oriana and Sumo turned and walked into the bank.

Winter ripped the red wig off as soon as she'd reached the side of the building. I took a deep breath of relief. Winter's long, dark hair tumbled all over her shoulders, as she ran—barefoot now—down the street, with Boges close by her side.

Suddenly the earpiece spluttered into life once more. 'We're out,' said Boges, as he ran. 'Any minute now the alarm is going to go off—once they realise that the safety deposit box is empty!'

Almost as he said the words, the alarm from the bank started clanging. I ran after my friends. Within seconds, police cars were converging on the street.

12 Lesley Street

12:02 pm

'That was way too close for comfort!' said Boges, leaning over a chair and puffing.

Winter shook her head as she pulled off her jacket and practically ripped off her stockings. 'It was a close call,' she said, 'such a close call. But we did it! Can you believe it? It worked!'

All three of us jumped up and high-fived each other.

Boges threw himself on the couch, grinning. 'After what we've had to do to get this far, getting to Ireland will be a cinch!'

I didn't exactly share Boges's confidence, but at least we'd retrieved my family's heirlooms. Our quest could start again!

'Here,' said Winter, passing me the packet from Oriana's safety deposit box. 'You should be the one to open it!'

Winter and Boges leaned forward as I emptied out the contents of the package on the table.

The three of us stared in disbelief.

'Huh?' said Boges. 'What's that?'

'I don't believe it!' Winter cried in distress.

Instead of the amazing, one-in-a-million Ormond Jewel, we were staring at an ordinary oval brooch with a polished grey stone in the middle. I grabbed up what I first thought was the Riddle, only to find that it, too, was a fake.

'Look, *all* the edges are frayed,' I said. 'It's a copy! It's a good copy, but it's a fake! The original has a clean cut at the bottom–it's not frayed on that bottom edge like this one.' Slowly, I sank against the counter, all the excitement and energy drained out of me.

'They're not here,' said Winter. 'I can't believe

this! After everything we've done—Boges, all your work on the fingerprint. Disguises. Getting the PIN. I can't believe it.'

The moments ticked by with the three of us in stunned silence as we stared at the fakes in front of us. I tried to focus.

Something occurred to me. 'Oriana went to all the trouble of stashing them in the bank vault. Do you see what this means? Oriana doesn't know these are fakes! Someone else has the real Jewel and the real Riddle!'

Boges glared at me. 'If she doesn't have them, then who does?'

I looked at Winter, who suddenly seemed uncomfortable.

'It has to be Sligo,' I said. 'Somehow he must have intercepted my backpack at the funeral parlour and done the switcheroo. Oriana takes what she thinks is the original Ormond Riddle and Ormond Jewel and she stashes them in the bank for safekeeping, not realising that what she has is worthless. Worthless!' I said, shoving the fakes off the table with a sweep of my arm. 'Either there's a third party involved in this—someone we've never heard of and don't know about—or it has to be Sligo.'

'But why would Sligo do a switcheroo?' said Boges. 'He'd just take them, wouldn't he? Why go to the bother of replacing them with fakes?'

'So that Oriana would believe that she had them,' I said. 'That gets her off his back. She thinks she's sweet with the goods, leaving Sligo to relax and get on with the next part of his plan.'

Winter, who'd been sitting on the floor quietly, piped up. 'Or Rathbone has outsmarted them both,' she said.

'All my time spent in the fume cupboard in the science lab . . . all for nothing!' shouted Boges. 'And it worked, can you believe it? My fake print fooled Zürich Bank's scanner! *But what for?*' Boges stood up, shaking his head, and started pacing the room, tearing away all remnants from his Sumo outfit. 'We have just over two months left to sort this all out, and we're back to square one. Again!'

Winter looked from Boges to me, her face concerned and serious. 'What are we going to do now, Cal?' she asked. 'We can't give up. We just can't.'

Disappointment seeped into every cell of my body. I didn't know what to say.

'Let's think,' she said. 'We have to spy on everyone we suspect. I can increase my visits to Sligo's place. The weather's warming up, so I could start going round to use his pool. Maybe you two can watch Rathbone some more.' Winter glanced up at Boges who had slowed his pacing. 'You know what? Maybe we need to forget about *this* for a while,' she said, waving her hands over Oriana's fakes, 'and focus back on old leads—the drawings, the words of the Riddle—things that we may have overlooked. We can't give up. *I* won't give up.'

23 OCTOBER

70 days to go . . .

Hideout
38 St Johns Street

10:21 am

I figured I should give Winter a break, so I was back at St Johns Street. I felt helpless and angry, like I'd been kicked in the guts—except the kick kept on kicking. We were back at square one. Worse, if there was some third party we didn't know about, we were seriously behind the eight ball.

My phone started ringing.

'Cal,' Boges began, 'I have some information for you. Can you meet me at Winter's tonight? Bring everything you have—I think I know why your dad drew Caesar on the Sphinx drawing.'

12 Lesley Street

7:01 pm

'Come on, Boges, don't hold out on us,' begged

Winter. 'Where does Caesar fit in?'

'Patience, patience. All in good time.'

Slowly he pulled out his notebook, snapping the rubber band that held it together a couple of times before finally opening it. He cleared his throat and began reading: 'One of the simplest codes in the world is the Caesar shift–'

'A code?' I repeated. 'There's a code called the Caesar shift?'

'You betcha.' Boges snapped the notebook shut. 'I won't read the rest of it. Nobody really knows if Julius Caesar ever had anything to do with it, but anyway, that's beside the point.'

'Tell us how it works, already!' said Winter.

'It's coming, it's coming,' said Boges, pulling out a large piece of butcher's paper and picking up a pencil that was on the table. Very quickly, he wrote out the alphabet.

'It works like this,' he explained as he started writing the alphabet out again, but this time he began with the 'A' written directly under the 'B' of the previous line, writing the final 'Z' back under the 'A' in the top line of letters.

'That's a one-letter Caesar shift. So using the code, DBU becomes CAT. Get it? You can move it along as many places as you like. For instance, you could move the code along ten places and start your new Caesar code alphabet underneath the letter K of the original alphabet.'

Again, Boges wrote out the alphabet, placing the A underneath K. 'Now,' he demonstrated, 'CAT becomes SQJ.'

'Well, what are we waiting for?' asked Winter, excitedly. 'Let's try it! Let's apply the Caesar shift to the Riddle. But do we try a one-letter shift, or two, or three? And where do we start? Do we apply it to every word?'

'Yep,' I said. 'We should try every word and every shift—all twenty-six combinations.'

'I could probably design a program to work it out for us,' Boges said. 'It could take a little while, but once it's done, it'll crunch the combinations in no time. Then we can search through the results for another message within the Riddle. For information embedded in it.'

'What if,' I asked, 'the embedded information is in the last two missing lines?'

Boges shrugged. 'Could be. You know what we have to do . . .'

'Go to Ireland?' I asked.

'Go to Ireland,' Boges repeated. 'We need to talk to the Keeper of Rare Books, find out whether he really has information on the last two lines. Time's running out, we can't wait around for answers to fall into our laps.'

I looked around at the drawings. We'd finally discovered the existence of the Caesar shift—but was that what Dad was trying to tell me about? And Winter had matched the drawing of the little monkey with the painting of the young Queen Elizabeth—but was the Queen what Dad was trying to show us? Or did the monkey have more meaning?

'By the way,' said Boges. 'Gabbi told me that they were all going away this morning—Rafe and your mum have taken her down to Treachery Bay for a couple of days. For a break from the city . . .'

'Really?' Immediately I was interested—Rafe's house was where I'd first seen the scribbled note about the Ormond Riddle. 'That could be a perfect opportunity,' I said, 'for a thorough search of the place. Rafe could have information that we don't know about. Even Mum might have something incidental of Dad's that could mean a lot to us.'

'You took the words right out of my mouth. I'm in,' said Boges. 'I guessed you might want to check it out, so I already told Gabbi—our new little spy—that we might "pop in" in their absence. She's so cool,' he said. 'Straight away she switched into top-secret mode. She's left the key out for us and she said she'd turn off the CCTV system and sensor lights. We just need to remember to turn it all back on again before we leave.'

I grinned. I was so proud of my sister. She was turning into a handy ally.

Rafe's House
Surfside Street, Dolphin Point

9:30 pm

Boges and I ducked into the front garden, crept around the side of the house and onto the back patio, where we found the key Gabbi had left us under the barbecue. The night was dark and an eerie wind was blowing, but knowing the house was empty had made us both pretty relaxed about breaking in.

Next door's cat, who'd saved me last time I was here, rubbed our legs as we unlocked the back door.

I was ready. We were looking for anything—anything at all—that might give us more information about the DMO, and even if we didn't find anything, we'd at least be sure that we'd eliminated every possibility from the 'home' quarter.

We stepped through the double doors with torches that we kept low, directed to the floor. I hesitated once I stepped inside. A lamp had been left on and, somewhere, a radio chattered softly. Mum had always done that when we went away, to make it seem like the house wasn't empty.

'What is it?' Boges asked.

'Not sure,' I said, slowly walking into the living area. 'I can smell Mum's perfume, I think.' I spotted some familiar cushions and a rug from our old house. 'Maybe it's just Mum's stuff.'

The scent of perfume got to me. It was making my chest ache, reminding me of happy, easy times. Times when I felt safe.

'Sorry, what did you say?' I asked, realising Boges had asked me something, twice.

'Is that the smell you remembered catching a whiff of?'

'What do you mean?'

'The scent you caught a whiff of before you were attacked at the funeral parlour—you said it was a familiar smell.'

'No,' I said, firmly.

Boges didn't look convinced. What was he trying to say?

'It wasn't this smell, OK?'

'OK. So where should we start? Here in the kitchen?'

'Yep, you give that a go. Remember to check above the fridge, and I'll try over here,' I said, moving further into the living area and squatting in front of the low cupboards that ran along the wall, underneath the TV and sound system. 'Keep a lookout for any unusual documents and any plastic storage bins with red lids, like the one we found in the mausoleum back in January.'

10:37 pm

We worked silently and methodically, carefully going through every shelf at floor level, then standing and searching the mid-section of each room, before reaching up and tackling the high cupboards.

We moved through the ground floor, room by

room, including the study where I'd first seen that phrase scribbled in my uncle's handwriting: 'The Ormond Riddle?' There'd been a big clean-up in the study since last time. The drafting board and shelf tops were bare.

In the small, windowless room down the back of the hall, which had mostly been used to store gardening stuff, I found three of Rafe's red-lidded containers, all on top of each other.

I closed the door, switched on the light, sat down and pulled the containers towards me. I lifted the lid off the first one and began going through it.

I don't know what I was hoping to find, exactly, but I was disappointed when nothing sparked my interest. The files inside mostly contained diagrams of complex protein and carbohydrate chains, botanical and chemistry notes—stuff I'd seen back in January. Other than that, there were a few wads of old receipts and tax returns. Nothing to do with the DMO.

The door behind me opened and I looked up to see Boges's expectant face.

'Nothing,' I said, closing the containers and pushing them back into their original positions. 'You?'

'Nope. Nothing. I think we've covered the ground floor,' said Boges. 'Upstairs?'

At the top of the stairs Boges went one way, and I went the other. The first room I approached was Gabbi's. I stood in the doorway and slowly took everything in.

Boges had told me, a while ago, that Rafe had converted two rooms into one—an entire wall had been taken out—so that Gab's medical equipment could easily fit when they brought her home for care. But now, without the hospital stuff taking up space, it looked like Gab had herself the bedroom of her dreams.

She had a new big four-poster bed with one of those canopy things on top, with soft, white fabric falling down from it—the kind of bed you'd see in a story about a princess. In one corner stood a floor lamp that looked over a pink beanbag and a mountain of cushions, next to a long bookshelf filled with her favourite stories, and a small desk. A plush rug sat in the middle of the room, and on the wall opposite her bed was a wide wardrobe and an ornate, white dressing table with a frameless mirror and matching chair tucked in front.

A million memories seethed through my mind as I noticed more and more familiar things. The well-loved teddy bears and dolls on Gabbi's bed reminded me of a hundred stories.

Stuck on the mirror above her dressing table,

I found the funny cat cartoon I'd drawn and flown through her window. Impulsively I grabbed a black texta from a pencil case on her desk and added a top hat and curly moustache to the cat's face. That would make her laugh.

'Cal,' called out Boges. 'Check this out.'

I followed Boges's voice down to the far end of the hallway. 'What is it?'

'Look around you,' he said, shining his torch over the room we were in.

I did as he said and my jaw dropped.

It was my old room! It wasn't exactly my old room, because we weren't in Richmond anymore, but it was like my room had been picked up and carried here exactly as it had been. Suddenly I had this massive urge to just run and dive into my bed, wrap my old quilt around me, hug my pillow and shut my eyes.

Boges grabbed my shoulder, stopping me. 'No, dude. We don't want them to know we were here. Don't touch anything. Just remember what we're here for. You can't take anything from this room, OK?'

I looked around at my things and frowned. A photo of me—my last school photo—sat on top of my pillow like a sad reminder. Every little thing I could see helped make up the pieces of me that were missing. The pieces of who I used to be.

But Boges was right. I couldn't even take some fresh clothes out of my drawers.

'I'm going to head for Rafe's room,' I said to Boges, as I walked away. I had to stay focused.

The place had changed a lot since I'd been

snooping through it way back in January. I found where Mum must have been sleeping—previously a spare room—recognising her hair brush and perfume bottle next to a messy pile of letters on the dressing table near the door. But the room looked strangely uninhabited, as if rarely used.

I flicked through the letters—mostly old ones from Dad, sent from his work travels overseas—and found an airline ticket near the bottom. It turned out to be Dad's return ticket to Ireland, I realised, noticing the surname and last year's date. Because of his illness, he'd been flown home as a medical emergency, and then hadn't used the return fare paid for by his company—who were clearly expecting him to recover—because he *never* recovered.

Before I could think too much about it, I shoved it in one of the side pockets of my backpack, figuring no-one would know. It was some small link to Dad, and I wanted it.

Beside Mum's perfume bottle stood another with a typed label on it, as if from a pharmacy. From what I could make out it was some kind of herbal tonic.

Lastly, Boges and I focused on Rafe's room. Quietly we searched through drawers and cupboards, but our efforts weren't producing anything worth noting.

Just before leaving Rafe's room, I checked under the bed and found something that hadn't been there before. I pulled the green suitcase out and opened it. It was jammed with endless botany notes. I sighed.

I lifted out a few of the folders and glanced through them. I was faced with more pages of diagrams about linked toxin proteins in different classes of bracken ferns. Nothing about the Riddle or the Jewel. Nothing about my family. I unfolded a faded piece of drafting paper that was almost stuck to the bottom of the case, and flattened it out on the bed.

It was a house plan. Across the top, in typed letters, the plan read: 'Requested by: Tom and Winifred Ormond', and over the top of that was a stamp that read 'SALE APPROVED'.

Sale approved? I didn't recognise the house—it definitely wasn't our home in Richmond. My eyes scanned for some sort of familiar detail, but all that caught my eye was a red cross in one of the upstairs bedrooms.

I wasn't there to look at house designs, so I folded it back up and returned it to the suitcase, then pushed it back under the bed.

It was then that I noticed something else under there, on the floor on the other side, near the bedside table. Mum's beaded slippers.

Mum's slippers?

I stood up, confused, and turned to Boges. Suddenly Mum's old blue dressing gown came into focus, hanging on the back of the bedroom door.

'Are you OK?' asked Boges, staring at me as I shone my torch on Mum's beaded slippers. 'You—um—noticed the slippers and the dressing-gown?' he said awkwardly.

'She can't be sleeping in here,' I said in disbelief. 'She can't be. Right?'

'I'm afraid it looks that way,' Boges replied, frankly.

My mum was sleeping in the same bed as Rafe? It couldn't be true. I was suddenly dizzy. I didn't want to think about it.

'We've wasted our time. There's nothing here,' I said. I realised Boges was clutching a small card in his hand. 'What's that?'

'I found this in the rubbish bin downstairs. In Rafe's office. It was right down the bottom with a whole lot of other stuff on top of it.'

He handed it to me. It was Ryan Spencer's bus pass, the one I'd written 'Who am I?' on, and left in the letterbox.

Had Rafe found it in the mail and chucked it? Or had Mum thrown it away?

'Better put it back where you found it,' I said, handing it to him, but not before noticing that

Ryan's birthday was next month. I heard something outside and tensed up.

'What is it?' asked Boges.

'I heard someone pulling up in a car on the road outside,' I said. 'I'm going to take a look.'

I went down the hall and looked out into the front garden from upstairs.

I ran back to Boges. 'A car with its headlights off has just pulled up in the street outside.'

'They must have seen our torchlight. Let's get out of here.'

We raced downstairs, knowing we would have to leave by the back entrance to avoid anyone coming in the front. Could it be Rafe, Mum and Gabbi coming home early? But why the stealthy approach, without lights?

Once on the ground floor, Boges tinkered with the security system—setting it up to restart in five minutes. We ducked out the back way, and returned the key to where Gabbi had hidden it. Keeping close to the wall, Boges and I slid around the corner.

Nothing stirred. No car followed. Maybe I'd overreacted.

24 OCTOBER

69 days to go . . .

7:32 am

cal + boges, meet me at the clock tower, asap! winter.

Clock tower

8:21 am

I saw Winter before she saw me. Her wild hair was blowing in the wind and although she didn't seem to wear so many drifty, floaty things these days, her boots and her way of walking made her stand out. She saw me and ran over to me, the locket—the one I'd helped her get back from her thieving ex-friend—jiggling on its chain.

'What's wrong?' she asked. 'You look wrecked.'

'Big night last night,' I said, and quickly filled her in on the raid on Rafe's house and the search through Mum's stuff. Then I noticed Winter's eyes, and how anxious and fearful she was looking. 'What's wrong *with you*?'

'Boges will be here any second,' she said. I could read in her face that she was dying to tell me something. 'We may as well wait for him.' Right on cue, Boges appeared at the top of the clock tower stairs. 'There he is,' she said, waving to him.

Once the three of us had huddled together in a quiet spot, Winter began to explain the urgent meeting. 'Listen,' she said. 'I can't give you much information just yet, but something really big is going down. With Sligo and his crew.'

'You think he has the Riddle and the Jewel?' I asked.

'I'm not sure about that,' she said, 'but something's happened to change him. He's racing around organising this big, last-minute meeting—a business banquet. He's really on edge. I have to be very, *very* careful around him. Anyway, he's never organised anything like this before. Something's up.'

'Maybe he wants to make a big splash—announce what *he has*?' Boges suggested. 'Get his name in the papers—in the social pages?'

Winter considered this for a few moments. The three of us were leaning across the parapet that ran chest high around the lookout.

'Apparently he's been on the phone practically non-stop, talking to people, organising the event.

From what I've overheard I have the impression that he's trying to establish a connection between himself and Oriana de la Force.'

'Oriana? But they hate each other,' I said, frowning, remembering the way he'd spat on the ground at the mention of her, the first time I met him. 'Why?'

She shook her head. 'Maybe he wants to do a deal with her.'

'Yeah,' agreed Boges. 'If he has the Jewel and the Riddle, he might want to get together with her so that the two of them can work on the Ormond Singularity. He already knows she's his rival in this investigation, and there are little more than two months left. Or maybe he wants to team up with her so that they can both go after their common enemy.'

I pushed off the parapet and turned to Boges. 'Common enemy, meaning me?'

'Meaning you.'

My friends' faces were very serious. 'You really do seem to stand in the way of what they want,' said Winter. 'It's quite clear that you're the heir to some mysterious inheritance. For them to take it, you need to be eliminated.'

I swung round and looked out to sea.

Winter kicked some leaves away from the ground and sat down, cross-legged. 'After you two left last night I went over there,' she said, 'for a "swim". I heard him ordering all this food from a caterer—entrees and mains, chocolate mousse puddings, wine and liqueurs—the whole works. When he got off the phone I asked him what the big occasion was, but all he said was that it was a very important meeting between two very important parties. Then I made a joke about him becoming a society hostess, and that's when he involved me—he asked me to act as a kind of co-host to help him with it all.'

'Wow, he must really trust you,' I said, 'to ask you for help with something like this.'

'Guess so,' she said, staring at her boots. Did she feel guilty because he trusted her?

'He might want to make Oriana an offer,' I suggested. 'Find out just how badly she wants to get the Riddle and the Jewel back. How much she's willing to pay for them.'

'Sligo would never offer them to Oriana. He's determined to crack the truth about the Ormond Singularity. That's his *mission*. It has to be because of something else.' She looked at me and I could see fear in her pale face.

She probably had fair reason to be fearful. Oriana was a beast, capable of unimaginable terror. But did Oriana know that the Jewel and Riddle—the contents we stole from her safety deposit box—were fakes? If so, she'd be thinking that Sligo had just stolen them from her. But if Sligo had the *real* Riddle and Jewel, he must have intercepted them—stolen them—back at the funeral parlour.

'I read a book about Chicago gangsters,' began Boges. 'They used to pretend to reconcile with their rivals and then they'd organise a big celebration dinner for them. Just when everyone was relaxing, eating and drinking, the machine guns would start going off! Maybe Sligo's setting her up to get rid of her.'

Winter shook her head. 'If Sligo was going to get rid of Oriana, he'd do it quietly. Why chuck a party and make a great big song and dance about it in his own home, with all those witnesses? No way. That's not his style at all . . .'

Boges and I exchanged curious looks. Again Winter looked like she had more to say but was holding back.

She caught us glancing at each other. 'Look, I've always known Sligo's a bad guy, but sometimes you hope so bad for things to be different that you almost make it happen in your head. Anyway, a visit to the car yard overnight quickly demolished my stupid dream of Sligo ever really changing.'

'What happened?' Boges and I asked.

Winter sighed before speaking. 'After I left Sligo's I made my way to the yard. I was sneaking in when I saw Zombie Two pacing up and down, on the phone to Sligo. I could tell because he was all "yes boss", "no boss", "anything-you-say boss". Then, after he hung up the phone he went over to the oil tank . . .'

'*The* oil tank?' I repeated.

'Let her talk,' said Boges. 'Go on, Winter.'

'He unscrewed the lid, reached in . . . and after a bit of fumbling . . . he dragged out a body.'

We were stunned into silence.

'It shouldn't come as a surprise to me *or* you,' she said to both of us. 'It could have been you, Cal, who he was fishing out. We all know what Sligo's capable of, which makes the idea of him getting together with Oriana really scary. I'm worried about what might happen at that dinner. I mean, anything could happen and I don't want to get caught up in it. Being there makes me part of it, and I do not want to be part of it.'

If Winter Frey was admitting she was scared, she must have meant it.

'But then,' she said after a pause, 'being there could give me a chance to gather information—I'm sure I'll overhear something that will help us with the DMO.'

'So you're going to do it?' I asked, surprised.

'Yes. I'll do it for two reasons. One I've just told you—the intelligence gathering exercise.'

'And the second one?'

'The more I cooperate with him, the easier it is for me to get along with him. The easier it is for me to get along with him, the easier it is for me to keep looking for the evidence *I* need.'

'Evidence?' asked Boges.

'I want to go back to the car yard, find my parents' car again and thoroughly check it over. I also want to accept that my parents had good reasons for leaving so much of their wealth to Sligo, and for leaving *me* with him. I need to see their wills for myself. There's this part of me that can't believe they'd cut me out like that. But then again, Vulkan can be really charming when he wants to—and they could have believed he would be the best guardian for me.'

She sat close beside me, her head down, fiddling with her locket.

'I was hoping,' she continued, 'that sometime during the banquet, when Sligo's busy "entertaining" his guests, I might get a chance to go through his office—see if I can find copies of my parents' wills.'

'If you're co-hosting,' I said, 'it's going to be hard to slip away without anyone noticing.'

'I know,' she sighed. 'Oh, that'll be Miss Sparks,'

she said as her phone vibrated in her pocket. 'Back in a sec.'

She wandered away to take the call and I quickly turned to Boges. 'I have an idea,' I whispered to him.

He shuffled along the ground, closer to me. 'Let's hear it.'

'We've bugged Oriana's office before, and we could do something similar at this banquet.'

'With Winter's help?' he asked. 'Is that what you're saying—set her up with a wire?'

I nodded silently to my friend. He thought about it for a second, then he slowly nodded, too. 'We can do better than that. How about if we could *see* as well as hear? How about we use a spycam? We could fix it somewhere hidden—they're only small. I reckon I could fit it into her locket,' he said slowly, looking over to where Winter was standing, still on the phone. 'If I can get one of the new really tiny spycams.'

I saw the two worry lines on Boges's forehead flatten out and his eyes get rounder as he caught hold of the idea and ran with it. 'Dude, it's all possible! We can sneak pictures as well as audio so that we see and hear everything that goes on. Just so long as Winter stays in the room.'

'Boges, that would be awesome.'

'Cool. Let's do it.'

'Here,' I said, surreptitiously peeling out some money from my gold stash in my backpack. I palmed it to him. 'Winter's locket,' I said. 'That might be the tricky part.'

'I'll leave you to deal with getting that off her, buddy.'

Just a few metres away, Winter hung up her phone. She jogged back to us. 'I have to bolt,' she said. 'Miss Sparks is already waiting for me at my place—I had to make our study session earlier.'

'Hang on, please don't tell me the banquet's on tonight,' I said, catching a frustrated look appearing on Boges's face.

'Sure is,' she said, as she picked up her bag. 'I told you it was last minute. I'll call you in a couple of hours—Sparks will be gone by midday.'

As soon as Winter disappeared down the stairs of the clock tower, Boges pulled out his mobile phone. 'We're going to have to move fast,' he said to me. 'Seriously fast.'

We both looked at the screen of his phone as he logged on to a surveillance specialist's website. Within a few minutes, we'd seen the range of pinhole camera lenses housed in front of tiny radio transmitters, capable of delivering sound.

'I could make this even smaller—get rid of the housing and use Winter's locket as the housing,' said Boges, pointing to the screen where he'd zoomed in on the smallest of the range, 'and then just drill a tiny hole in the front of it for the lens. I know a guy I can get this sort of gear from. I'd better go see him now and tell him what I need.'

'Winter won't like the idea of you drilling a hole in her locket.'

'I'll hide the wire by running it through the chain of the locket,' Boges continued, taking no notice of what I'd just said, 'then down the back of her neck under her gear. We tape the leads into the battery and tuck it into her waistband. I'll direct the audio and video feed to my laptop, and then we sit in the next room—'

'Whoa,' I said. 'It's at Sligo's place, remember? I don't think we can *sit* in the next room.'

'You have a point,' he said, resigned. 'That'd be dangerous.'

'You don't say. But we will need to set up somewhere close. We'll be able to see and hear any plans they make. Catch any mention of the Riddle and the Jewel. We might find out who has them and if there's a chance for us to snatch them back.' I was beginning to feel hopeful again.

12 Lesley Street

12:11 pm

'No way!' yelled Winter, spinning around to face

me. 'You want me to wear a camera and microphone into that banquet? That's insane! How am I going to explain that if I'm sprung? Tell Sligo I'm practising to be a reporter? Doing a project on journalism? Next they'll be dragging *me* out of the oil tank!'

'Let me explain,' I said. 'Boges can customise a really small spycam. Nobody will see anything. I'm talking *micro*.' I pinched my thumb and forefinger together to make a minuscule space. 'A tiny spycam and a tiny transmitter—so small they'll fit inside your locket. We'll only need to drill—'

'*Drill?*' Winter's hand flew to her chest and she grasped the locket. '*My* locket? Forget it! You're not touching this!' Winter's face wrinkled up in fury. 'How could you, Cal?'

'It was just an idea,' I said, pulling out my mobile. 'See? Look at the size of the lens on my mobile's camera.' I pointed it towards her. The lens winked like a small, black bead. 'See what I mean? And the one we have in mind is even smaller.'

Winter stormed away and plonked herself on the couch. She pulled her knees up, and turned her face away from me. I watched her as she held her locket and opened it, staring at the pictures of her parents inside.

A memory of her face suddenly flashed into

my mind—I recalled the way she had lovingly held the locket after I helped her get it back, in February. We were practically strangers then. We were friends now. How could I have asked her to damage something that meant so much to her? I'd need to find something else.

I walked over to the dressing table. Hung over the mirror, together with a couple of scarves and a long rope of pearls, was a crystal necklace, a gold pendant on a chain and a string of chunky, brown wooden beads. I picked up the beads. They were about half the size of walnut shells, and seemed hollow.

'They'll work,' said Winter, from behind me.

'These wooden beads?'

'Yes,' she said, taking the necklace from me, and placing it around her neck. 'Yep, they'll work,' she said with conviction. 'You'd better call Boges and tell him I'm in.'

'Are you sure?'

'We have to take risks for what we believe in. That's what my mum and dad always told me.'

3:21 pm

Old leaves and bits of newspaper whirled around in the corners of the rooftop as I waited for Winter and Boges to turn up. Winter said she'd be back from Sligo's at three, but was running late. She had gone there to gather as much information about the party as she could. Boges had managed to buy the spycam we needed from his contact, but was frantically trying to get his tools together and back to us in time to carry out the rest of our plan.

4:00 pm

Convinced my friends weren't going to show up any time soon, I went back into Winter's flat and parked myself in front of the TV. It flickered to life just as Winter flew through the door.

'Sorry I'm late. Boges is right behind me,' she said, holding the door open with her hip. Moments later Boges appeared, red-faced and sweaty. 'It's OK, guys,' she continued, 'the banquet's not on until late—nine pm. We still have time. Quick, to the table.'

Leaning over a bowl of pretzels, Winter began telling us everything she could about the night ahead.

'Sligo is using the big downstairs living area for his banquet,' she said. 'He's hired tables and dining chairs, which he's set up all in a line. I offered to lay the tablecloths and arrange the flowers—that's why I was so late—so I'm in his good books right now. The caterers have already begun preparations in the kitchen. He's taking it very seriously. Remember how I told you about the New Year's Eve Council Ball that he wants to host? I think he's considering this as some sort of practice run. He wants me serving drinks outside in the gardens around the pool terrace from about eight thirty.'

Boges nodded. 'Any good suggestions as to where we can set up the observation post?'

'I think the safest place would be the pool shed where the pool chemicals and garden tools are kept. It's only new, so it's pretty empty at the moment. It's always locked but I can make sure it's unlocked, and before the guests arrive, you guys could set up in there.'

I looked at Boges and nodded. 'Sounds good,' I said. 'Plus we're not too far away from you, in case things get—well—messy.'

'Let's try not to think about that happening. I'm so nervous,' said Winter, holding up her two hands in front of her. 'Look, they're shaking.'

I grabbed both her hands with mine and they felt really cold. 'You can do it,' I told her.

4:29 pm

In less than half an hour, Winter's small apartment had been turned into a technical workshop again. Boges's tools were spread all over her table and an extension lead for his drill snaked along the floor.

Winter and I watched as Boges used a tiny drill to bore through the back of the brown, hollow bead that hung in the centre of Winter's necklace. He drilled an even smaller hole in the front, for the camera lens, then fitted the spycam and its minuscule microphone into the round space behind it.

Next Boges threaded the wire through the existing holes in the beads on the necklace, concealing it almost completely.

'There,' said Winter as she fastened it around her neck. 'How does it look?'

'I can still just see the microphone wire,' I said. 'It needs to be invisible.'

'You can see it because you're looking for it,' said Boges. 'Winter, you'll have to wear a jacket or something to cover the wire going down your back, and tuck the battery into your waistband. We'll tape everything down, so nothing comes loose. When you're ready we'll give it a test run.' Boges hoisted his laptop out of his backpack. 'You flick that small button on top of the battery pack to activate the spycam.'

Once Winter was ready for the test run, she disappeared through the front door, closing it behind her. Boges and I waited inside, tensely staring at his laptop screen.

Suddenly the screen came to life. The world of

the roof outside Winter's flat appeared in grainy, monochrome grey on the screen. The familiar cityscape and timber flowerpots came into view, all moving as Winter moved, like images from a black-and-white film.

'Cool!' I said, patting Boges on the shoulder.

'I hope you guys can hear me,' Winter's voice came through the built-in speakers on the laptop.

Then she must have turned, because the camera jerked a little and panned around. Now, instead of the cityscape that we'd been looking at before, we saw wind chimes and her front door coming closer and closer with each step she took towards it. Then the door opened and we could see ourselves on the screen.

'Could you hear me?'

'Clear as crystal,' I said, grinning.

Boges stood up and carefully gave her a hug.

'OK,' she said, 'now I'd better tell you guys how to get in.'

7:43 pm

My stomach was churning with nerves as I sat next to Boges, both of us dressed in black, on our way to Sligo's. I'd called on Nelson Sharkey for help, and he agreed to drive us and provide us with a quick getaway. I was gritting my teeth and trying really hard not to think about what we were about to do. If I thought too much about the danger we were willingly putting ourselves in, I would have thrown up.

'OK, guys,' said Sharkey, slowing his car and pulling over a few hundred metres down the road from Sligo's house. 'This is as far as I want to go. I'll be waiting here for you when you come out.'

'*If* we make it out,' said Boges.

I looked through the window and saw that we were parked out the front of a vacant lot. It would probably be developed soon and turned into an almost-instant homestead like Sligo's. Up on our right was the café Repro and I had met Winter in before we stole the Jewel from Sligo's safe. Further up the street was empty of parked cars, which I hoped meant no visitors just yet.

Boges and I climbed out in the twilight, carrying our backpacks behind us. We scurried along the street and disappeared down a lane at the rear of Sligo's property. Winter had promised us that the security would be concentrating on the entrance of the house, leaving the backyard relatively unguarded.

I spotted the gate that Winter had left open for us, and we darted in, closing it again behind us. The layout was just as she had described—ahead of us was the long, glistening pool, lit up by underwater spotlights, and it was surrounded by a sweeping terrace, lined with glowing bamboo lamps, that led to the house. There was movement inside, but from our position we couldn't make out exactly who was there.

A few steps from the back gate stood the pool shed, a solid construction of timber that matched the decking. The shed door was slightly ajar. We slipped inside, closing it quickly behind us.

Boges turned to me and swore. 'I can hardly breathe,' he whispered. 'What are we doing in here? This is Vulkan Sligo's backyard!'

'Too late to back out,' I said. I was thinking exactly the same thing, but needed to keep it together. 'We'd better set up.'

A small window let in just enough light to see a stockpile of pool supplies stacked near one end of the shed. Other than that there was a leaf blower and a big pair of gardening clippers. That was it. We quickly rearranged some of the bags of salt to make a barricade for us to hide behind.

Boges opened his laptop and we stared at the screen, waiting.

Footsteps approached the pool shed.

'Someone's coming!' Boges hissed in my ear. He quickly shut his laptop as we ducked down.

The footsteps grew louder.

The door of the pool shed opened. We both lay pressed against the floor, the stink of a chlorine-like substance filling my nostrils. I could feel Boges trembling. Or was it me?

After a clattering sound the footsteps receded, the door banged shut again, and a few seconds later we could hear the leaf blower working outside.

'Last minute tidying up for the guests,' I whispered. We both remained frozen, knowing that the leaf blower would be returned to the shed shortly.

After a few minutes the drone of the blower fell silent and we heard a voice shouting out from the house. I was sure it was Sligo. 'Pour another bag of salt in the pool, while you're at it!'

Boges and I looked at each other in horror. Anyone coming in to drag one of the bags of salt we'd used to hide behind would find us.

'What are we going to do?' Boges hissed, clearly starting to freak out. 'What difference is a bag of salt going to make right now? The guy's nuts!'

The footsteps approached again.

'We'll just have to overpower him!' I said. 'We have the element of surprise on our side. We'll jump him and tie him up! Cover his mouth with–'

The door opened again and we flattened ourselves even further, but this time I was ready to pounce.

Whoever it was stepped inside the shed and

stowed the leaf blower away noisily. Then we heard a grunt, like the sound somebody makes when they sit down with relief.

What was going on? The guy wasn't moving. He sure wasn't grabbing a bag of salt from the supplies. I took a long, silent breath and peered out.

It was *Bruno*! And he wasn't doing anything! He was just sitting there—taking a breather! Here, out of sight, he thought he could have a bit of a break from work!

It might have been a relaxing moment for him but it sure wasn't for me and Boges! With my face to the floor, stray grains of salt and dust were irritating my nose.

Oh no! Not a sneeze coming on! *I mustn't sneeze!* I pinched my nostrils, desperately trying to ward off the sneeze that was building in my sinuses. Boges glared at me, willing me to hold it back.

It was like a scene in a bad movie—the sneeze was welling up and there was nothing I could do to stop it. Any second now, I'd sneeze and he'd be right on us. We'd be captured!

The pool shed door was suddenly wrenched open. 'Bruno, what are you doing in here?' came Winter's sweet, life-saving, voice. 'The boss is looking for you! He's not happy!'

Bruno groaned again and hurried outside, slamming the door behind him. The sound of the door covered the sneeze that had finally, uncontrollably shot out of my mouth. I rolled over in relief.

'Bruno is *Red Singlet*, right?' said Boges. 'I thought he was in jail!'

'He should be! He must have some seriously good legal connections. Winter must have been watching the shed and came down to get rid of him.'

'Just in time, dude. Just in time.'

8:39 pm

The noise from the terrace was increasing as more and more guests arrived. From the shed, Boges and I could hear scraps of conversation and the clinking of glasses.

Once the guests moved inside the house, the yard became very quiet and we relaxed a bit.

'Has she come online yet?' I asked, impatiently looking at the screen. 'She could be missing something important.'

'She'll switch it on once they're all seated. Just wait.'

9:05 pm

The screen of Boges's laptop remained empty.

'Are you sure your program is OK?' I asked him, anxiously. 'Surely she should be coming through by now.'

'Chill, dude. Everything is ready and waiting. All Winter has to do is flick the switch—'

It was as if she'd heard Boges's words, because the screen suddenly lit up to reveal Sligo's living room and his guests, milling around the long table that ran up the centre of the space.

'There they are!' I said. 'We're in!'

Some of the guests were already sitting at the table, which was decorated with a huge bunch of red waratahs and white pillar candles in the centre, and lines of table napkins spreading like fans down either side. Others stood chatting in small circles.

We could hear Winter's voice, offering to pour more drinks or invite people to eat a canapé.

'There's Sligo!' said Boges, as the hidden camera turned suddenly, revealing him seated at the head of the table. He was talking on his mobile while Bruno—with his hair slicked back and wearing a suit jacket over his red singlet—sprawled beside his boss, watchfully scanning the group.

The camera moved closer to Sligo. 'Winter's doing really well,' said Boges. 'Moving nice and steadily. Giving us some nice close-up shots.'

'Oh, no,' I said as the camera approached Sligo's other companion. 'It's Zombie Two! What if he recognises Winter from the car yard?' The camera swerved away quickly, then returned to Zombie Two, as though Winter had done a double-take.

We waited, tense and fearful, as we heard Winter offering him a drink. I watched his face intently on the screen, looking for any signs of recognition, but he barely looked up as he took a glass of red wine from her tray. I heaved a sigh of relief.

Soon it seemed that everyone was seated and waiters appeared carrying steaming bowls of soup.

'There she is,' said Boges, indicating the intimidating presence of the criminal lawyer, Oriana de la Force, as she sat down a few seats away from Sligo. 'Check out the hair!'

Her red hair was swirled up like a big pile of spaghetti, and pinned down with some sort of feathery fascinator—like girls wear to the races—which almost looked like a bird had dive-bombed and crashed into her bun. We couldn't see the colour of the dress, but I guessed it was purple—that seemed to be her favourite colour. It had a strange collar like a shelf that ran all the way around her shoulders.

Sumo sat beside her, fiddling with Oriana's silver cachous box, picking it up and dropping it back onto the table. There was no sign of Kelvin.

Oriana snapped, snatching the box from Sumo, making him jump.

'Hang on,' said Boges, suddenly alarmed.

'What is it?'

'Isn't that Sheldrake Rathbone,' he added in surprise, 'sitting next to Sligo like he's his right-hand man?'

'You've got to be kidding,' I said, squinting at the screen. But then, sure enough, the slimy solicitor came into focus, wearing a flower in his buttonhole and a smirk on his face. 'They must be working together! What a *creep*! I should have known he was in deeper than he let on!'

At that moment, Sligo handed Rathbone a wooden box, like a cigar case. There were too many voices overlapping and I couldn't understand what he was saying. Just how involved was Rathbone?

'Did he just say something?' I asked.

'Patience, my friend,' said Boges. 'At this stage, they're all just making small talk. They'll settle down in a minute. Hang on,' said Boges, sounding even more shocked at someone's presence. 'Isn't that Murray Durham sitting there? Murray "Toecutter" Durham?'

'So it is,' I said, cringing. 'He doesn't look too healthy. And he's with his bodyguard–the guy who lives in the house Winter and I broke into to get back her locket!'

The men at the table were all dressed in suits, but there was no hiding the tattoos that snaked up their necks, or the scars that disfigured their hands—these guys weren't as clean cut as they hoped to appear.

'I can't believe the crims that are here,' said Boges, 'all gathered in one spot. The hornets' nest. And here we are, spying on them, hiding in the pool shed out the back!' he said with an uncomfortable laugh.

For a while, all we heard were the sounds of people eating and drinking and the occasional laugh, but none of this came from Sligo, Oriana or Rathbone. Whenever Winter's camera panned to their faces, they looked very unhappy.

'Winter's in a really good spot,' I said, noticing how she'd joined the guests at the table now, and had positioned herself in such a way that we had most of Sligo on screen and about three-quarters of Oriana. 'She's good and close to the two people we're most interested in. The two deadly enemies having a meal together. I just hope she's sitting close enough for us to hear them talking. If Sligo's planning some massacre, like Al Capone,' I said, 'we'll have it all on video . . .'

Oriana's diamond earrings flashed as she moved to eat from her steaming plate. Sligo's bald head moved from left to right as he spoke to his sidekicks. Then he leaned closer, towards Oriana, who was speaking to him.

Everyone seemed to hush all of a sudden.

Boges and I looked at each other with excitement because we could hear every word.

'I'm willing to do a deal with you, Vulkan,' she said. 'I'm willing to work with you. We both want the same thing. Together, we'd make a brilliant team. I must say, although I was absolutely livid at first, I was impressed with the way you did it. I didn't realise you were so intelligent. Hiring actors to impersonate me and my bodyguard—what a riot! I've been underestimating you all these years.'

Sligo pulled back, a frown on his face. His green cravat puffed up like a pillow under his double chin. He put down his wine. 'Hiring *what*?'

Boges and I exchanged a split-second glance before returning, captivated, to the screen.

'One day,' said Oriana, 'you'll have to tell me how you hacked my fingerprint. But tell me now, how on earth did you obtain my PIN?'

From the look on Sligo's face, it was obvious that he thought Oriana had lost the plot.

Boges and I looked at each other open-mouthed. 'She has no idea it was us!' I said. 'I'm not even on her radar!'

'Oriana, my dear,' said Sligo, trying his best to remain composed. 'What are you talking about?' His pouchy face compressed in an angry frown. 'What actors? Impersonating who? PIN? Hacking?

What absurd allegations are you making now? Have you gone completely barking mad?'

'Vulkan, *darling*, there's no use denying it. I viewed the bank's security tapes myself. They were quite convincing. Although I'd never use that shade of lipstick.'

'Lipstick? I'm trying to make a deal here with you, and you're raving on about actors and lipstick! Am I wasting my time? Why must you continue to be so—' he paused, searching for the right word, '—difficult?'

'Difficult?' shrieked Oriana. '*I'm* being difficult? What game are you playing now, Vulkan? I should have known better about coming here tonight! You always were impossible, and you haven't changed!' She banged down her glass on the table, sending red wine splashing all over the tablecloth like blood splatter. Sumo leaned in to mop some of it up with a napkin, but Oriana smacked his hand out of the way. 'Leave that, Cyril,' she ordered.

The camera shifted up for a second, like Winter was getting out of her seat.

'Sit down,' said Sligo, and the camera returned to its former position. He turned again to Oriana. 'I could say the same thing about you, my dear. You're being impossible right now.'

'Don't you "my dear" *me*! Don't patronise me,

just because you have the upper hand.' Oriana's voice became coarser—even more threatening. 'I know a lot about you, Vulkan Sligo. A *lot*,' she said, exaggerating her point with a wide gesture. 'I could do you a *lot* of damage. People talk, Vulkan. I know what you're really like. That cravat can't cover up the blood you have on your hands.'

Sligo pounded his fist on the table and everyone fell silent. 'How dare you accuse me! You don't know what you're talking about!' he said, his face reddening with every word.

'I'm a businesswoman,' Oriana continued, unwavering. 'I know you didn't throw this banquet for my pleasure. You maintain the stronger position at the moment, I am aware of that. I thought I had secured . . . well, I *believed* I had secured the goods in question, but then you just came along and helped yourself to them.'

'Oriana, who are you trying to fool here?' interrupted Sligo's angry voice. 'I *know* you have the damn things. Quit the act! That's why I invited you here tonight—so that we could come to some sort of arrangement. Something that would benefit both of us. I wouldn't like any injury to befall you, but I'm afraid that could happen if you don't cooperate with me.'

'Are you threatening me?' Oriana's voice was razor sharp.

Boges frowned. 'What's going on? Why is Sligo playing hard to get?'

'The only thing that would be beneficial to me right now,' said Oriana, 'would be for you to acknowledge that you stole the Riddle and Jewel from me—'

'*You* stole them from *me*, you thieving, lying witch!'

I grabbed Boges. 'Man, this is unbelievable! She thinks he has them—'

'—and he thinks she has them!' Boges finished. 'Dude, what a head-spin! And if *we* don't have them, then who the heck does?'

This was intense! Someone else was involved! Someone we didn't even know about! A million crazy possibilities whirled through my mind.

Back on the laptop screen, an expressionless man in a suit suddenly walked up behind Sligo, leaned down and whispered something in his ear. I could just make out Rathbone, beside him, squirming in as Sligo relayed the information to him. Sligo's brow was covered in sweat. Suddenly he stood up and charged over to Oriana, and practically dragged her out of her chair.

Sumo pounced, trying to tear Sligo off her.

'This room is bugged!' Sligo screamed, finally releasing his grip from Oriana. 'My chief of security has just informed me that someone is wearing a wire!' With that, he swung around to Red Singlet, seizing him by the shoulder. 'Bruno! Search the place! Everyone up! This banquet is over!' He swung round to Oriana once more. 'If you've bugged my house—'

'Me? Bugging this function? It's not me who's done this!'

All of a sudden the images on the screen went berserk, swinging wildly from side to side, before the screen on Boges's laptop went black.

Silence.

'Winter!' I said to Boges. 'What if someone realises she's the leak?'

'I don't know, dude! This is not good!'

Impulsively I opened the shed door, about to run out to her.

'What are you doing?' Boges hissed, grabbing my arm and jerking me back inside. 'It's no use going and getting the two of us caught as well!' The shouts from the house were audible now, even from where we were in the shed. 'Sit down!' Boges yelled at me. 'We just have to wait it out! There's nothing we can do right now. Everyone's leaving—this would be the worst time for us to go out.'

10:31 pm

It took quite a while, but as soon as the noise

from the house had settled back down, the two of us fled the shed, ran through the back gate, pounded down the lane and around the corner to the main road.

We ducked down at the sight of Oriana and Sumo on the street being hustled by security into the dark blue Mercedes. Sumo's shirt had been ripped open—they must have searched him for a wire. The car doors slammed, then the Mercedes accelerated noisily and sped away.

Now the yard and the street outside were empty. The other guests must have exited pretty quickly. There was no sign of Sligo himself. Or of Winter.

I didn't know what to do. If Winter had been discovered, spying on two of the biggest criminals in the city . . . Dread and horror seized me as I thought of the filling oil tank, and her trapped inside it.

With Boges beside me I ran across the road, pulling my hoodie around my face, headed for Sharkey's car. Something caught my eye on the footpath and I stopped to pick it up.

'What are you doing?' asked Boges, skidding to a halt.

I showed him Winter's bead necklace. It was broken, some of the beads were missing, but it was still threaded with the fine wire from the spycam. The tiny lens remained in place but the leads and the battery were missing. Had Winter managed to ditch everything herself or had Sligo ripped the spycam and its battery from her neck?

'Over here, Cal! Boges!'

Ahead, Winter leaned out of the back of Sharkey's car and waved. 'Quick! Jump in!'

The two of us dived in and Sharkey slammed the accelerator, speeding us out of there. It was a tangle of bodies as the car seemed to accelerate from zero to one hundred in a nanosecond.

'You're OK!' I said, straightening up in the back seat beside Winter, while Boges climbed over the centre console and into the front.

'Of course I am,' she said, buckling her seatbelt. 'Sligo's so furious he didn't even notice me slipping away. Nelson, can you please take us to my place?'

'Sure thing,' said Sharkey. 'Boys, you OK?'

'Yeah, yeah, we're fine,' said Boges. 'Awesome job, Winter. The spycam worked perfectly.'

Winter gasped, clutching at her chest. 'It's gone!'

'Here,' I said, showing her the broken string of beads I picked up from the yard.

'Thank goodness I didn't leave that behind. You can have this back,' she said, reaching round behind her skirt and peeling the battery pack off her skin, before handing it to Boges.

'So what happened?' I asked. 'Last thing we saw and heard was Sligo yelling that the place was bugged, then the camera started doing somersaults.'

'It was chaotic,' she said. 'I was sweating bullets, thinking they'd somehow trace it to me. I sure didn't want to be found spying on my–' she spat the words out, '–my great benefactor! But everything was so wild that it gave me the perfect opportunity to disappear upstairs.'

'To Sligo's office?'

'Yep, Sligo's office. So did you hear?' she said, and I wondered if she was changing the subject on purpose. 'Sligo doesn't have the Jewel *or* the Riddle! Neither of them do! Can you believe it?'

'Wow,' said Sharkey. 'Someone's outsmarted them both. But who?'

'We don't know.' I wound down the window for some fresh air. 'My money's on Sheldrake Rathbone.' Sharkey's eyes questioned me in the rear-vision mirror. 'Rathbone was there,' I explained. 'Sitting next to Sligo like he was his advisor.'

'It's a good guess,' Boges said, zipping up his bag. 'Rathbone has the means. He also has access to a lot of information. He could have done the switch at his brother's undertaking business–taken the Riddle and the Jewel out of Cal's backpack and substituted the fakes to be collected by Oriana's team. She was fooled—she thought she had the real things stolen out of the bank. Remember, only a few people know what they actually look like.'

12 Lesley Street

11:28 pm

Inside Winter's flat, the two of us sat side by side on the couch. Sharkey was dropping Boges home.

'Our next move has to be a search through Rathbone's place,' I said.

'Winter?' I asked, when she didn't reply. 'Have you fallen asleep on me?' I gave her a little nudge.

'Sorry, sorry,' she said, stretching out, 'it's just been a long day. You were talking about Rathbone, yes. Search his home or office?'

'Both. Although I'm pretty sure we won't find anything buried in the yard after springing him red-handed that night. Maybe we should try the office first.'

'That's not going to be easy. I could always help you with Sligo's premises, but getting into a solicitor's office isn't going to be easy. Especially when it's in the Pacific Tower building.'

I leaned back, thinking and sipping hot chocolate. 'Maybe I could approach him in a straightforward kind of way,' I said. 'Tell him I want to turn myself in—come clean about everything—that I'm sick of life on the run, and need his help.'

'But Cal, if he's the one who has the Riddle and the Jewel, he doesn't need you. What can he gain from meeting you?'

I shook my head. 'There are still some things that he doesn't have, and that he needs to know about the DMO. Like the missing two lines of the Riddle, like the link to the Keeper of Rare Books at Trinity College in Dublin. He doesn't have the real drawings and he doesn't know about the transparency with G'managh and Kilfane on it. I can use those to keep him interested.'

'Maybe,' she said. 'So were you worried about me?' she asked. 'When you and Boges were hiding out in the shed.'

I nodded. 'Of course. We both were.'

'That's nice of you,' she said, playing with a loose thread on one of her cushions. 'So nice.'

'Are you OK, Winter? You sound a bit funny or something. What is it? What's on your mind?'

'Oh,' she groaned, snapping the thread and tossing the cushion aside. 'It's this.'

She pulled a small writing pad out of her shoulder bag and threw it on the table in front of me. It landed with a clap. 'I found it at the bottom of one of Sligo's office drawers.'

I picked it up and looked at the first page of the pad. It was blank.

'Go to the end of it,' she said. 'The last three or four pages.'

I did what she said and found that the last three pages were covered in signatures; the same signature, repeated over and over.

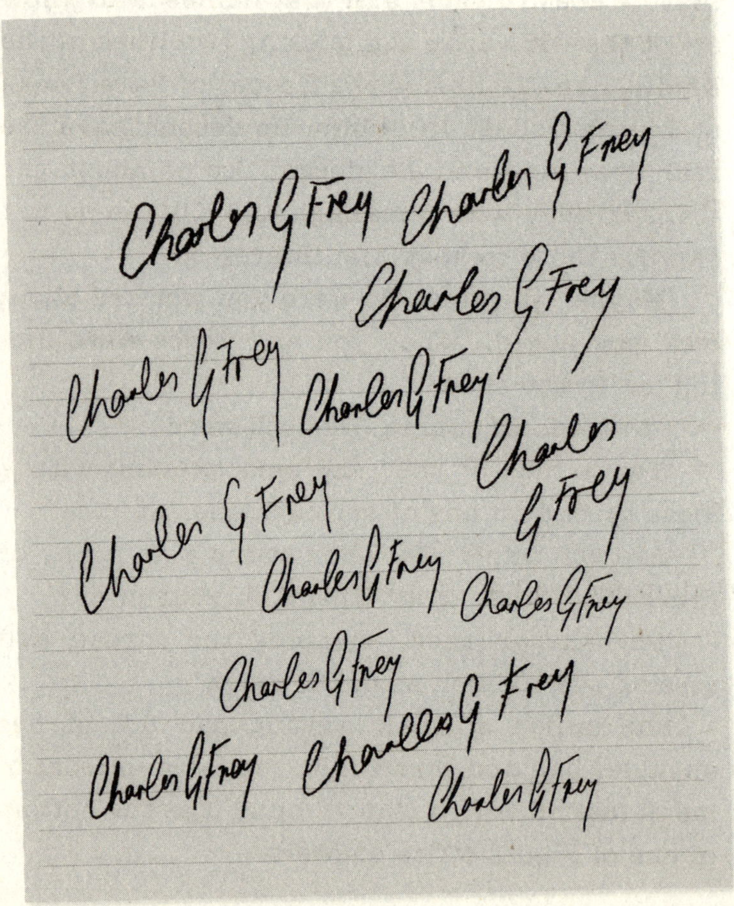

I looked up at her, puzzled. 'Your dad?'

She nodded. 'His surname was originally "Fong" but he changed it to Frey when he moved to this country. Charles G. Frey.'

I carefully examined the signatures. The first few were shakier than the later ones. I looked into Winter's dark, troubled eyes.

'So it wasn't your dad practising his signature, it was Sligo.'

'Exactly,' she said, solemnly.

'And there's only one reason why Sligo would have practised your dad's signature,' I said.

'Forgery,' she said.

'Forgery,' I repeated.

Winter stared blankly at the floor. Everything seemed darker all of a sudden, like the moment immediately after a candle's blown out. I wanted to say something to her—something that would make her feel better—but nothing would come to me.

Finally she pulled her legs up onto the couch, curled up, closed her eyes and drifted off to sleep.

25 OCTOBER

68 days to go . . .

9:20 am

'Rathbone will be out of the office between twelve and two today,' Winter announced as she shook me awake. After she'd fallen asleep on the couch last night, I'd draped a blanket over her and crawled into her bed. It was funny waking up and looking at the flat from another perspective.

'How do you know that?' I asked as I rubbed my eyes.

'Easy. His receptionist just told me. I rang his office to make an "urgent appointment" with him, and this super-chatty lady picked up the phone and went on to tell me how he was in this morning but he'd be ducking out for a meeting at twelve, and then he'd be back at two, but wouldn't be able to see anyone because he had a bunch of conference calls to take with—wait for it—his associates who are currently interstate!' Winter paused to take in an exasperated breath. 'Cal, the office is practically empty!'

'This is too good,' I said, climbing out of bed. 'What time is it?'

'Half-past nine. Get ready, and let's go.'

Pacific Tower

11:55 am

Rathbone trotted out of the building and hailed a taxi around a quarter to twelve. As soon as he was gone, Winter and I made our way inside and up the lift to level five. Winter told me to stay behind for a minute while she took care of the receptionist. I had no idea what she was planning as a distraction, but had to trust her. She turned and winked at me as she approached the glass doors of suite two.

My hands were sweaty and the parcel I was carrying, again in an effort to look like a courier, felt warm and awkward. I fumbled with my phone as I waited, keeping my head low.

There were only two businesses on level five, an accounting firm on the left, and Rathbone & Associates on the right. In the foyer between the two, in front of the lift, was a sleek, black leather lounge. I put the package down beside it, then bent down, pretending to tie my shoe, while I peered through to the reception area. Winter was talking to the woman behind the counter. From the large nameplate on the reception desk I could just make out her name as Dorothy Noonan.

'Yes, I've always known that I want to be a solicitor,' I heard Winter say. 'I thought it would be a good idea to try and get some experience, while I'm still a student, and visit some local firms to see if anyone would like my help after school, a couple of afternoons a week.'

A smile grew on my face—we were becoming experts in subterfuge. I checked no-one was looking, and made a hasty crawl through the doors, directly past Winter's legs and the reception counter. My sudden confidence was quickly taken down a notch or two when I realised Rathbone's personal office was walled in by glass—I'd be completely exposed.

Silently, I stood up, opened the glass door and stepped inside. Moving like a ghost, I crept behind the desk and crouched down.

I began working my way through the drawers, looking for any secret compartments, big enough to contain the Jewel and the Riddle. I could feel the sweat returning to my forehead and trickling down my back as I searched. If anything went wrong, and Rathbone came back early, I knew I'd be in the hands of the police within minutes. That's if Rathbone didn't do away with me first. He was a mysterious guy—who knew what he was capable of?

A few minutes had passed and I hadn't found anything. I hoped Winter would be able to keep the 'chatty' receptionist occupied. I snuck a look to check what was going on.

I could hear laughter! 'Oh, love, I know,' I heard Dorothy say. 'When I was about your age I did some work experience in a cosmetic laboratory and it was exactly the same!'

I had no idea what they were talking about, but all that mattered was that they were still talking.

I was searching Rathbone's shelves, checking behind dozens of books, when my fingers encountered something metallic. I dug around and pulled it out. It was a small, metal box with a key left in the lock. I turned it and the lid opened. Inside was an envelope addressed to Sheldrake, with Irish stamps on it.

Letters from Ireland to Sheldrake Rathbone!

I skim-read the letter and one word jumped out at me: Graignamanagh. The letter was from someone in Graignamanagh, Tipperary, Ireland. *G'managh* had been marked on the transparency from Dad's suitcase!

'I'll just photocopy it for you, love,' came Dorothy's voice, as she suddenly walked into view.

I dropped to the floor, but accidentally knocked over a glass filled with pens and pencils!

'What was that?' asked Dorothy, quickly approaching Rathbone's desk.

'That's nothing,' I heard Winter say. The pair were now standing in the room with me, as I huddled under the desk. 'Look, Dot, how about I clean this up while you make the photocopy?'

'Thanks, pet. Sheldrake likes his desk tidy.' I watched the floor as Dorothy's feet walked away again.

Winter dropped to her hands and knees, and picked up the stray pens and pencils. Her face suddenly met mine. 'Get out,' she whispered. 'Rathbone's on his way back already and I can't keep this up for much longer! Plus I can't let Rathbone see me! What if he recognises me? What then?'

'Did you say something, love?' Dorothy called out.

'No, no, I'll be out in a sec,' said Winter, standing up and returning the glass to the desk. She left the room.

I was getting out from my hiding place when I banged my head and looked up to see what I'd hit. It was a metal lever. What was that doing there? It looked like some kind of handle. I backed out then pulled down on it as hard as I could. Something clicked then whirred. Then, from under the desktop, a large drawer descended.

A secret drawer! I felt around, trying to work out how to open it, my hands trembling and fumbling in my haste. I finally found another small handle, which I pulled. The drawer slid open, revealing one very fat file. I blinked. 'Ormond family genealogy', I read.

Feverishly, I hauled it out, shuffling for more light as I flicked through its contents.

Rathbone must have been gathering information on my family for decades! There were handwritten histories from generations ago, and family trees following the descendants of Black Tom's son, Piers Duiske of Duiske Abbey. There were letters from solicitors and lawyers from Ireland. I fumbled all the contents back into the folder, knowing that I'd have to scram, and as I did this, my eyes fell on some lines in one of the letters: '. . . too difficult to access all the coded information, it is suggested instead that a search through the remnants of any forts or houses built by the tenth Earl in the area of Carrick on Suir, be undertaken instead. In this way, we cut the Gordian knot, avoid wasting time with decoding and move straight to searching possible locations.'

My fingers shook as I tried to silently squeeze

the file back into its secret compartment. I couldn't work it out and was running out of time, so I left it in its lowered position and crawled out backwards from under the desk.

I looked out and saw Dorothy fussing over the photocopier. She was still rattling on about something as Winter nodded nearby. Winter caught my eye, and looked furious. 'What are you doing?' she mouthed, desperately. 'Get out!'

It was a risk, but there was something else I wanted to do. I re-opened the filing cabinet containing Rathbone's clients' records, and began flicking through the names. I skipped ahead to the surnames beginning with an 'F'. It was a crazy idea, but Rathbone and Sligo were clearly in cahoots, so I needed to make sure that there wasn't a file in there concerning the Frey family—Winter's family.

There was a Fredericks, a Freeman and a French, but no Frey. I glanced over at the photocopier again and Winter was staring at me. 'I'm going!' she mouthed again. This time she ran a finger across her throat to emphasise the danger.

I heard the lift coming. Was Rathbone on his way up? But then, like a bolt of lightning, another idea came to mind. My fingertips scrambled along the tops of the files, flying over more surnames. Fisher, Fitzpatrick, Foley, Fong . . .

Fong! Charles G. Fong! I almost couldn't believe my eyes as I wrenched the file out and shoved it into my backpack.

I thought I could hear the lift stopping at the floor below so I raced to the door. Winter was gone, and I could see Dorothy typing away at her desk. A single scrunched-up ball of paper in the rubbish bin caught my eye. I grabbed it, shoved it into my pocket, then fell to my knees, crawling, once more, past reception.

I heard the lift locking into position on this floor. I had to move fast!

I scampered through the foyer and past the lift, just as it opened. I stood up and ran into the neighbouring accountant's office, throwing myself down on a chair in their waiting room. I watched through the doorway as Rathbone stepped out of the lift and into his office, but not before he threw a sideways glance my way.

'How may I help you?' asked a man in reception.

'Oh,' I said. 'Sorry. I think I'm on the wrong level.' With that, I got up and hurried to the lift.

I swore when the lift was suddenly called down to the ground floor. I hit the down button, taking sideways looks at Rathbone's office, wondering how long it would take him to notice the hidden drawer's position.

I jiggled with impatience, listening to the lift

doors opening downstairs and to the silence coming from Rathbone's offices. I prayed this would continue a while longer.

Come on, *come on*, I muttered to the lift through clenched teeth, hearing its doors close downstairs, and the whining of its ascent to the first and second floors.

A sudden eruption of sound came from Rathbone & Associates. I heard loud cursing and then suddenly Rathbone appeared behind the double glass doors, heading straight for me, one fist raised in the air and his face contorted with rage. The lift doors opened and I jumped in, punching the 'close doors' button.

'You! Come back here, you little thug! You *criminal*!' he shouted.

The lift doors started to close. Hurry, *hurry*! I begged them.

Rathbone stuck one foot in the door and the lift doors parted again. He pulled them open with his hands, leaped into the lift and grabbed me round the throat. 'What did you take?'

'Nothing!' I said struggling to free myself as the lift doors closed and we started descending. 'Get your hands off me!'

'We'll see about that!' he said, tightening his grip on me. 'I'm marching you straight down to the police. You've blackmailed me once, but that won't scare me again. This is the end of you. You'll be locked up and they'll throw away the key. You'll be an old man by the time you get out! And do you know what? I'll be enjoying all the wonderful things that the Ormond Singularity brings me while you're rotting away in some maximum security prison. In fact, once I have my hands on it, I'll send you a postcard.'

Rathbone was surprisingly strong and although I struggled vigorously, he was able to keep a tight hold on me as the lift doors opened onto the ground floor. What happened next seemed like something filmed in slow motion. Winter, wearing a blonde bob wig, and Boges materialised on each side of the doors as they opened. They exploded into the confined lift space, hurling themselves on Rathbone, hoisting him up in the air.

'Get out of here, dude!' Boges yelled.

'Disappear!' shouted Winter. 'We can handle this!'

I gave one last violent, twisting squirm, wrenching myself right out of my hoodie. Meanwhile, Rathbone struggled and swore, pinned in the corner of the lift by my two friends.

I ducked past two people who were waiting for the lift—they jumped backwards in shocked surprise.

'Stop him! Stop that boy!' Rathbone yelled,

kicking and struggling. 'It's Callum Ormond! Psycho Kid!'

'Go, dude!' Boges shouted. 'Just go!'

I hated to leave them like that, but I had no alternative. I did as Boges ordered and ran like the wind.

12 Lesley Street

2:45 pm

I didn't know what to do but head back to Winter's house and nervously wait for my friends.

I pulled out the crumpled piece of paper that I'd taken from the rubbish bin near Rathbone's desk and smoothed it out.

It was a list of words—names of some sort—with the first three crossed out.

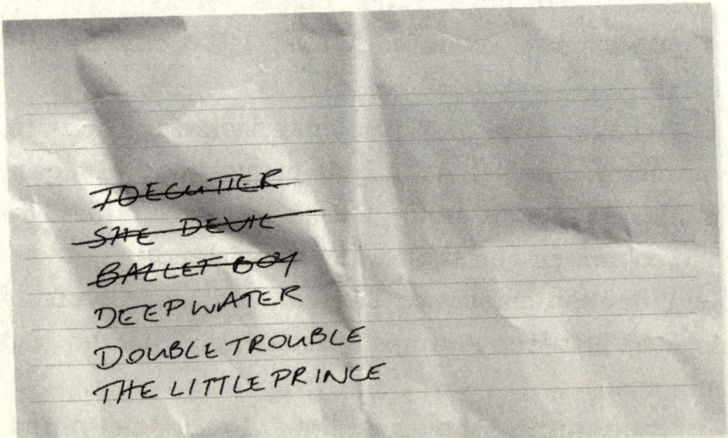

'We're back!' shouted out Winter, as she and Boges appeared at the door. 'Poor Rathbone had no hope against this,' she said, as the two of them posed, flexing their biceps. 'But seriously, how could you leave me with Dorothy for that long? She was sweet, but that lady can talk your ears off. I hope it was worth it. Did you find anything?'

'You bet I did! The guy has a file on my family as thick as two telephone books! He's been gathering information for decades—he has a genealogy of the Ormond family starting way back! He probably knows everything about it.'

'Did you find anything to do with the Riddle or the Jewel?'

'Nothing like that. But there was a letter from Ireland, from Graignamanagh—like that name on the transparency. Plus I found a weird list of names, screwed up in the rubbish.'

'Anything else?' asked Winter.

'Yeah, something else.'

'Well, what is it? What did you find?'

'I found a file with your dad's name on it. His real name.'

'What?' she said, her face turning pale. She slowly sat on the couch, her skirt billowing like a cloud. 'Did you see what was inside?'

'I thought I'd leave that to you,' I said, reaching for the file that was squashed into my backpack.

Her eyes lit up with excitement and reluctance. I handed it to her. She held it gently and cautiously, as though any sharp movement would set it off like a grenade.

Boges and I silently watched as Winter read through the paperwork in the file.

'Is it the will?' I asked finally.

'Yes,' she whispered. She raised her eyes, and there were tears in them. 'It says exactly what Sligo told me it would say. He gets everything, including me. He has to provide me with guardianship, take care of my expenses and provide me with an allowance. It's all there.'

'It's all there?' I asked, confused, staring at my friends in disbelief. 'But what do you mean? It's all legit? Sligo was telling the truth?'

'Not exactly. There's one thing that's very clearly *not* legit.' Winter held up the final page for us to see.

Boges and I both leaned in.

Staring back at us was a signature: Charles G. Frey. Some of the lines were shaky and lacking confidence. It perfectly matched the repeated signatures Winter had found on the notepad in Sligo's office.

'Forgery?' asked Boges.

Winter and I both nodded. I noticed now that she was smiling. The biggest, broadest, shiniest smile I'd ever seen on her face was beaming back at me. I could practically feel the surge of renewed energy rush through her. Her pale cheeks were now flushed with colour.

'I always knew something was wrong,' she said. 'They loved me. They didn't disinherit me. Sligo did that. They loved me, and I loved them. As soon as the DMO is sorted, I'll be taking all of this—the will and the signatures notepad—to the police.'

4:00 pm

Using my phone to jump online, I searched for the meaning of 'Gordian knot' while Winter went through the falsified will again in the kitchen, and Boges talked to someone on the phone outside. I read that there was a legend about Alexander the Great who instead of wasting time trying to untangle a famously complex knot, simply cut through it with his sword.

Rathbone had accessed all this information about the Ormond family because he was the family's solicitor. But his interest went much further than that. He too was trying to track down the truth of the Ormond Singularity and if we weren't careful, with his contacts and money, Rathbone could get to Ireland before us. He'd cut through the double-key code of the Riddle and the Jewel using the Gordian knot technique—he wouldn't waste time trying to decipher the secrets, he would just jump right in and take what was mine.

Time was running out. We were just three kids. But then I thought about how Boges and Winter had broken me out of Leechwood Lodge Asylum, how they'd tricked the biometric scanner at Zürich Bank, and how they'd hurled themselves at Rathbone, enabling me to escape. I realised we made a great team. We were much more than just three kids.

Winter handed Rathbone's list of names to me. 'It looks like nicknames,' she said. 'Coded names. And I think I know who the first three are.'

'Toecutter, She-Devil and Ballet Boy?' I asked.

'Everyone knows who Toecutter is. Sligo has started up an interest in the ballet,' she reminded us. 'He's going in for art—with a capital A,' she added, in her mocking tone. 'And there's one woman who instantly springs to my mind,' she said, 'when I hear the words "She-Devil"!'

'My thoughts exactly,' said Boges, who had been pretty quiet since coming back inside. He was stirring a pot of noodles on the stove. 'That's Oriana de la Force, all right.'

'OK,' I said, thinking hard. 'And they've all been crossed off. That doesn't look good—for them, I mean. Is Rathbone planning to have them rubbed out? Or do you think it means he's *ruled* them out.'

'Ruled them out—from what?' asked Winter.

'What everyone's after,' I said.

'The Ormond Singularity,' said Winter. 'And possession of the two objects that lead to it.'

'So he believes one of these three people,' I said, 'Deep Water, Double Trouble and The Little Prince, has them.' I thought a little more. 'But there's another person we can rule out from having the Jewel and the Riddle—Rathbone himself. If he had it he wouldn't still be searching for it. What do you think, Boges?'

Boges nodded, gloomily. 'That makes sense.'

'Boges, you OK? What's eating you?'

'Yeah,' said Winter, tossing her hair back. 'No offence, but you've been in a bit of a bad mood ever since we met up today.'

'Stop hassling me, both of you,' snapped Boges. The two lines on his forehead deepened, furrowing his face.

'Hassling you?' said Winter. 'I'm concerned, that's all!'

But he turned away, not wanting to take it any further. Maybe he was getting down about this endless quest for the truth.

Boges turned back. 'I can't take it,' he said. 'Cal, there's something I need to tell you—there's something bad happening. I don't know what to do. I don't know how to tell you.'

'What?' I asked, a sick feeling forming in the pit of my stomach.

'Dr Leporello contacted you.' An image of the freaky fungus expert, with his deadly toadstools and sickly skin, filled my mind. 'There was a message on your blog,' Boges continued, 'with a number to call. I've been wondering when might be the right time to bring it to your attention. But with something like this, there *is* no right time. I took the liberty of calling him.'

'When? Boges, you're scaring me. Has something happened to Gabbi? To Mum?'

Slowly Boges pulled a scrap of newsprint attached to a printout from his pocket. 'I'm sorry I'm only telling you now,' he said, passing the papers to me.

My heart was pounding as I took them from him, focusing on the torn-out piece of newsprint first. It was a wedding announcement.

WEDDINGS

ORMOND-ORMOND

Winifred Ormond and Rafe Ormond have pleasure in announcing their forthcoming wedding on October 31, at Chapel-by-the-Sea.

Shock made me blind for a minute. I read the words again. There was no denying them.

Mum was marrying Uncle Rafe! Confusion followed shock, leaving me speechless. I tried to process all the thoughts that were bouncing around my head.

I knew Rafe had been very good to Mum, helping her through my dad's death and all the mess that followed. He'd even offered to mortgage his house to pay for my legal defence—I knew he meant well even though I found him hard to get on with. But this wasn't right—it was too soon. No-one could take Dad's place.

Boges looked at me nervously. 'I'm sorry, dude.'

Then I read the printout. Now there was another addition to my confused feelings—fear and terror. I had to read it again, trying to control my racing emotions and mind.

'What is it?' Winter's voice cut through my confusion. I handed her both pieces of paper.

'Your mum and uncle are getting married? On Halloween?' She raised her eyes to mine. 'That's just days away.'

'Read the other bit—the printout.'

Winter started to read aloud. 'I have information from a very reliable source that a contract killer will be at the chapel. During the wedding, the groom—' She looked up at me and then at

Boges. 'Is this for real or somebody's idea of a sick joke?'

'Keep reading,' I said. 'Decide for yourself.'

'The groom,' she continued, 'is the target. The groom?' Winter repeated. 'Rafe?'

'I just called Leporello,' said Boges. 'He insisted that according to his underworld contacts, this is no idle threat. Rafe is in danger.'

The three of us looked at each other, exhausted by this news.

'He has to be warned,' I said.

'I already did that,' Boges said. 'Told him I saw something about it online.'

'And?' asked Winter.

'He just laughed it off. I told him about Leporello being a well-known police informant and your uncle said I'd been watching too much TV. He's not taking it seriously at all. He insists nothing will frighten him out of marrying the woman he loves.'

Hearing those words made me feel so uncomfortable. I wanted Rafe to care about my mother, but I didn't want him to marry her!

'This is serious,' I said. 'Maybe he'll listen to me.'

'You're kidding,' said Boges. 'Dude, get real. If he wouldn't listen to me, what makes you think he'll take any notice of you? He thinks you're deranged.'

'Why would Rafe be on the wrong end of a contract killer?' I said aloud, half asking myself. I remembered the gun I'd found in his bedside table, and remembered how he'd almost been killed in the January break-in.

Rafe knew he had enemies.

I had to get out, on my own, and clear my head.

7:22 pm

I walked along the beach, the waves roaring and crashing beside me. I hunched against the wind, my hands gripping the straps of my backpack, head down, fighting a sickening mixture of fear and anxiety.

Guilt gripped me as I knew it wasn't only the fear of my uncle's murder that was troubling me. Somewhere, deep in my heart, I still carried the hope of me and Mum and Gabbi living happily together again back in our house. It was this image that had kept me going all these months. It wasn't just solving the mystery of Dad's death and the DMO. The biggest reason I was trying to do this was so that I would have something to give to my family. Even without the threat of a contract killer, this wedding meant the end of my idea of home.

But if anything happened to Rafe, how could

Mum survive another sudden loss? She'd lost Dad, then me, then she'd almost lost Gabbi, and now came a very serious threat to another member of our family. The crazy guy had been right. The Ormond Singularity had caused nothing but death and destruction to my family. I had to do something to save Rafe.

I pulled out my mobile and dialled my mum's number. My hands were sweaty and hot.

'Hello?' she said.

Hearing her voice, a voice I hadn't heard for so long, hit me hard. 'Mum, it's me.'

'Cal? Cal, darling, is that you? Is that really you?'

I looked around as the lights along the esplanade suddenly came on, shining like stars in the grey light of the evening.

'Where are you? Are you all right? Cal, I've been so worried. You don't know what I've been through.' In her voice was the strange tone I'd noticed before, somehow flat, not like the voice she'd once had, which sounded full of life.

'I sent a photo to you—Ryan Spencer. And I asked you a question.'

'Ryan?' She asked, in a shaky voice. 'A photo of Ryan? Who's that?'

'Ryan Spencer. I sent you his bus pass . . . He's the boy who looks identical to me.'

'Identical?' My mum gasped, then the phone line fell silent.

'You there?' I asked. 'Did you get the bus pass?'

'What bus pass?'

She was stonewalling me. I didn't have time for this just now. I went straight ahead with what was on my mind.

'I just heard the news,' I said. 'That you're marrying Rafe.'

'Come home, Cal. Hand yourself in and we can talk about it.'

'I don't want you to marry him, but that's not it. I'm really worried about Rafe. Someone I know—a reliable informant—has told me that Rafe's life is in danger. That someone will make an attempt to kill him at the wedding.'

My mum gasped again.

'You mustn't go ahead with the wedding,' I pleaded. 'You mustn't go to the chapel. Please listen to me for a change.'

The phone line was silent again.

'Mum?' I asked.

This time she'd hung up on me.

I slumped against a rocky ledge. She must have thought I was calling just to stir trouble. The pain in my chest was overwhelming. I let my head fall between my knees and closed my eyes.

You have to stop them, said a voice in my head, as a seagull squawked above me.

I didn't have much time. A sniper needs a nest—a firing platform. I had to check out Chapel-by-the-Sea. I had to find the sniper's firing platform.

26 OCTOBER

67 days to go . . .

4:46 pm

I headed off for Chapel-by-the-Sea, and on the way called Boges. 'Boges, ages ago you were working on something and you wouldn't tell me about it—something about invisibility?'

'It's still in the development stage. I haven't worked on it for a while. You're talking about my Disappearing Dust?'

'That's the one. Tell me about it.'

'It's a combination of chemicals, stored separately in a large capsule, but with the help of a little ignition device they come into contact and explode, creating a dense, impenetrable smoke-screen. It works like a smoke grenade except it's a whole lot smaller and easier to hide.'

'That's what I need. I need to be invisible and I need to create a diversion.'

'Dude, I don't know how safe it is. I'm still working on the right amount of explosive for the detonation.'

'I have to stop the wedding,' I said. 'I have to save Rafe from the hitman. Somehow.'

'The detonator for Disappearing Dust is still very, very experimental.' Boges argued. 'I haven't tested it. I've been working on the Caesar shift code-breaker.'

'Boges, I have no choice. I need it. Please get it ready. The code-breaker will just have to wait.'

Chapel-by-the-Sea

5:27 pm

Chapel-by-the-Sea was a small, old-fashioned timber building famous for having the bell of a shipwreck in its tower. It sat on the headland surrounded by national park.

I'd been past it heaps of times whenever we'd driven with Mum and Dad along the coast. Once we'd even stopped there, and wandered inside the historic church, Gabbi and I climbing up into the choir loft to look down from high.

By the time I got there it was quite dark. I'd never broken into a church before and I wondered how I was going to do it until I noticed that the door was wide open. Cautiously, I moved inside. A woman was arranging flowers in vases on the altar, and she turned as I came in.

'I have to lock up in a few minutes,' she said.

'That's OK,' I answered. 'I won't be staying long. I have a school project,' I said quickly, whipping out a notebook and pencil, 'On historical church sites in my area.'

She didn't look completely convinced. 'You only have a few minutes before I lock up,' she warned, turning back to her work.

I looked around the church. There were some places to hide—shadowy niches with statues in them, the small side altar that was partly screened off. But it was much more likely the contract killer would just mingle with the guests, do the job, and escape quickly through the shocked congregation.

I turned around and looked behind me and up to the choir loft. The killer might wait up there, hidden behind the organ, only stepping forward to make the vital shot.

How was I going to prevent this from happening? And get out of there alive myself?

30 OCTOBER

63 days to go . . .

12 Lesley Street

8:20 am

'So the big day's tomorrow,' said Winter, as the three of us sat around, checking out the combat creations Boges had brought over for me.

'Tomorrow night, actually,' Boges corrected. 'It's an evening ceremony. It doesn't start until eight. There aren't many people going, but we were invited,' he said, explaining to me. 'Me, Mum and Gran. I figured we should go—it would be good for you to have me there—so I can keep an eye on Gabbi and your mum. Make sure they don't get caught in the crossfire.'

'I could come, too,' said Winter. 'I have this cream-coloured hat that I could wear—it covers half my face—so no-one will know who I am.'

'It's too dangerous, Winter,' I said. 'I think it's too risky at this stage for you to be recognised by someone. Who knows who'll be there. And you have your own family mystery to concentrate on.'

'That doesn't mean I want to quit helping you.'

'I know, but I'll feel better knowing I have one less person to worry about, OK?'

Boges handed me two objects cased in light metal, each about the size of a small carton of milk. 'Dude, please be very careful with these. I haven't completely figured out the explosive charge. If one went off near or against you, you could be badly injured. The idea is to throw them—like a grenade—and ideally not into anyone's lap. On impact, the chemicals combine and combust. The smoke is dense and almost instantaneous and covers a large area quickly. So you throw and you run—in the opposite direction, otherwise you'll get caught up in it too and you won't have a clue where you are. Or where anybody else is. Got that?'

I took them carefully from him and put them inside my backpack.

'And take this as well. It's another thing I have in the development stage—Special FX. I'm just not sure how much magnesium it needs. It works on similar principles as the Disappearing Dust, but this one makes a bit of a show with a big bang, big flame up and big smoke, but it won't hurt anyone. It might come in handy.'

31 OCTOBER

62 days to go . . .

Chapel-by-the-Sea

4:36 pm

Wearing a pair of grey school pants and a blazer that I'd picked up, I snuck into the chapel. The place was open, but empty. After spending fifteen minutes searching every possible hiding place, I was sure that the contract killer wasn't there—yet. I crept to the upstairs loft and crouched down beside the organ.

This month had been so full-on, so much had happened, that it felt like a year in itself. My brain was overloading with information. And now I was hiding out in a chapel, waiting for a contract killer to interrupt a wedding between my mum and my uncle! I took a few deep breaths and tried to concentrate on what I had to do.

6:00 pm

Marjorie and Graham, the next-door neighbours

from our old house in Richmond, were the first guests to arrive, bringing with them an elaborate sound system, and small bouquets that they hung on the ends of each pew. From my position, high up in the back of the church, I watched them as they set up the speakers. Good—that meant no organist.

Eventually guests started drifting in and taking their seats. There weren't too many, and most of them I didn't recognise, apart from a few people from Mum's old work. Boges walked in with his mum and his gran on either arm. He led them towards the front, to the side of the second row. That was the perfect spot to stay out of harm's way, but to be close enough to help my mum and sister, if they needed it.

8:10 pm

Soon everyone was settled, waiting for the bridal pair and Gabbi to turn up. All the time, my eyes were scanning the guests, constantly searching for something—anything—that seemed out of place. Wondering if I'd make it in time to stop someone raising their arm and taking aim.

As I looked along the first three rows of people, everyone looked normal, just like guests at a wedding should. They were seated quietly, occasionally turning to each other to say something in a whisper. How would I know what a contract killer looked like anyway? No doubt they'd have mastered the art of blending in to any group.

8:46 pm

They were really late. Everyone in the chapel was getting edgy, and the killer must have been amongst them.

Rafe suddenly walked up the aisle to the altar, alone, wearing a dark suit which I swear was one of my dad's. I visualised a small, red target on his head. He nodded to Marjorie, who was on standby, near the sound system. The sound of the famous wedding march music reverberated through the chapel as I clutched the canisters of Disappearing Dust and Special FX.

I peered over the top of the railing around the choir loft, and saw Mum walking up the aisle. She looked really thin and frail, and was wearing a pale blue dress that hung limply on her, accentuating her tiny frame. Gabbi held Mum's hand, and was wearing a ring of white flowers on top of her head that she kept adjusting.

Should I throw one now? I hesitated. I didn't want to make my move too late, but I also didn't want to do it prematurely.

As they approached the altar where the celebrant—a friendly-looking woman in a navy dress—waited, Gabbi pulled away sideways and slid into a pew and I saw Marjorie put an arm around her.

What if, I thought, I'm too late, and the contract killer fires his weapon and Rafe falls down—or worse—the killer misses, taking down Mum instead?

Rafe and Mum stood in front of the celebrant near the altar, looking at each other from time to time. The image of them together was making me feel dizzy. I had to focus.

A guy in a suit stood up and joined them, holding a cushion with a couple of wedding rings on it.

Now everyone was sitting still, listening to the words of the celebrant. She lifted her head and smiled as she spoke, looking around at the small group in front of her.

'And now,' she said, 'I'm required to ask—' she cleared her throat and in a louder voice said, 'if any of you gathered here before me this evening know of any reason why these two persons should not be joined together in holy matrimony, please speak now.'

From nowhere, a man, dressed in a long coat and a hat that hid his face from my view, stepped out of the shadows. Beneath me, this stranger reached in under his coat.

I sprang up and gripped the first capsule of

Disappearing Dust in my fist. 'Everyone! Look out! There's a gunman in the church!'

The stranger held a weapon in his hand.

I started racing down the stairs, and hurled the first capsule down into the body of the chapel. A massive cloud of thick, brown smoke erupted. I continued down the staircase, toward the mushrooming cloud.

As I hit the last step and jumped onto the floor, I heard my mum cry above the panicked screams of the fleeing guests. 'Cal! That's my son! Cal, where are you?'

I caught a glimpse of Boges briefly looking up in my direction. He'd already pushed his mum and gran out the door, and he had Gabbi's hand gripped in his.

People were screaming, and tripping over each other as they fought their way out.

Then the dense smoke took over and hid everything from my view. I had no idea where the gunman was. I hoped he couldn't line up a shot under these conditions.

'It's Ormond! He's here! He's trying to kill his family!' I heard someone cry.

I yelled out again. 'Everyone out of this church! There's a killer on the premises! Leave now!'

I thought I saw the contract killer's long coat swirling in the smoke near me, heading for the exit. Immediately, I lobbed the second capsule of Disappearing Dust up into the loft.

I threw myself out the back door just before the choir loft and the whole of the back wall of the chapel exploded in a supernova of flame and smoke. Boges had warned me it wasn't quite ready, and he was right about that!

From what I could make out, the chapel had now emptied. I bolted for the door and just made it outside as the whole back of the chapel wall collapsed. The timber side walls and parts of the ceiling caught alight, flames and sparks spiralled up in thick plumes of smoke, the back of the roof sagging at an angle, threatening to crash to the ground.

Guests were running clear of the burning building towards their cars, and safety. Among them I spotted Mum and Rafe stumbling along, followed by the celebrant. There was no sign of the gunman.

I had to get away. I'd been identified and already I could hear the sirens. From the direction of the city came the staccato *whoomp, whoomp, whoomp* of a helicopter.

Behind me, the fire burned furiously, crackling and spitting, with the occasional loud explosion as old timber and paint went up.

As I raced away, I took in my surroundings. Ahead there were suburban streets with houses on both sides and cars parked along the tree-lined kerbs. I needed to get away from this area. There were too many people—too many witnesses. I hoisted my backpack higher on my shoulders, put my head down and started charging along the footpath, glad that the night had well and truly closed in. People emerged from their houses to look back past me to the burning chapel that was lighting up the sky.

The sounds of the helicopter came closer. I was suddenly blinded by a brilliant light.

Desperately I ran faster, trying to get past the circle of light that fell on top of me. I ran and ran, but no matter which way I ducked and weaved, so did the helicopter. It kept right on top of me, following me with its spotlight. Trying to run from it was like trying to shake a shadow—impossible.

I raced under a tree and with eyes that were still dazzled, I saw what lay ahead of me. A huge semicircle of SWAT officers with shields and batons, were charging down the road, coming straight at me.

There was nowhere to run.

The police cars were bearing down on me on the road behind, while in front of me, the SWAT officers were advancing at a lethal rate. I'd saved Rafe from a fatal bullet, but stopping the wedding had put *me* in the line of fire.

I continued to run, squinting, trying to escape the relentless ring of the spotlight on me.

All of a sudden I remembered the third canister Boges had given me—Special FX! His new experimental noise-and-flash creation!

It was my only chance. I wrenched it out of my bag and threw it.

The canister rolled up in an arc, then back down again—a small, black silhouette against the unnatural bluish light streaming from the police chopper above.

It landed. Nothing happened.

The SWAT officers ahead stormed closer, as cops jumped out of their cars, ready to attack from behind.

I skidded to a halt. I had nowhere to go.

I stared at the canister, lying still on the ground. Boges's latest invention, Special FX, hadn't worked!

It was dead. Just like me.

CONSPIRACY 365

12 BOOKS 12 MONTHS

❑ BOOK 1

❑ BOOK 2

❑ BOOK 3

❑ BOOK 4

❑ BOOK 5

❑ BOOK 6

❑ BOOK 7

❑ BOOK 8

❑ BOOK 9

❑ BOOK 10

❑ BOOK 11

☑ GOT IT!

COLLECT ALL 12 BOOKS